T0121042

WHO GOD IS, AND WHAT HE REQUIRES

It's All About Obedience

WALT THRUN

WESTBOW
PRESS®
A DIVISION OF THOMAS NELSON
& ZONDERVAN

Copyright © 2021 Walt Thrun.

All rights reserved. No part of this book may be used or reproduced by any means, graphic, electronic, or mechanical, including photocopying, recording, taping or by any information storage retrieval system without the written permission of the author except in the case of brief quotations embodied in critical articles and reviews.

WestBow Press books may be ordered through booksellers or by contacting:

WestBow Press
A Division of Thomas Nelson & Zondervan
1663 Liberty Drive
Bloomington, IN 47403
www.westbowpress.com
844-714-3454

Because of the dynamic nature of the Internet, any web addresses or links contained in this book may have changed since publication and may no longer be valid. The views expressed in this work are solely those of the author and do not necessarily reflect the views of the publisher, and the publisher hereby disclaims any responsibility for them.

Any people depicted in stock imagery provided by Getty Images are models, and such images are being used for illustrative purposes only. Certain stock imagery © Getty Images.

Scripture quotations marked (NIV) are taken from the Holy Bible, New International Version®, NIV®. Copyright © 1973, 1978, 1984, 2011 by Biblica, Inc.® Used by permission of Zondervan. All rights reserved worldwide. www.zondervan.com The "NIV" and "New International Version" are trademarks registered in the United States Patent and Trademark Office by Biblica, Inc.®

Scripture quotations marked (NASB) taken from the (NASB®) New American Standard Bible®, Copyright © 1960, 1971, 1977, 1995, 2020 by The Lockman Foundation. Used by permission. All rights reserved. www.lockman.org

Scripture marked (KJV) taken from the King James Version of the Bible.

Scripture marked (NKJV) taken from the New King James Version®. Copyright© 1982 by Thomas Nelson. Used by permission. All rights reserved.

ISBN: 978-1-6642-4017-9 (sc)
ISBN: 978-1-6642-4016-2 (e)

Print information available on the last page.

WestBow Press rev. date: 07/28/2021

DEDICATION

This book is dedicated as a legacy to
my children and grandchildren.

Autumn Wine

A goblet flush with wine of spring
exudes hypocrisy
while new wine may delight the eye
there's much we cannot see.

Though vernal wine may boast the fruit
that's choicest on the vine
still such new wine will not prevail
when weighed with summer wine.

Yet summer wine still lacks in part
the excellence of bouquet
but passing of more time will birth
a priceless cabernet.

An aging wine is likened to
the seasons of a man
for wisdom finds a friend in him
whose years have greater span.

The man that's wise becomes as wine
refined of dregs and lees
for such a man will fear his God
refined of vanities.

But autumn wine as such is naught
without a primal reason
if it's not shared with those who walk
in spring or summer season.

So I delight to be to you
a fount of autumn wine
to share the riches given me
and fill your glass from mine.

Yea, to my heirs who follow me
I offer more than gold
the treasures in my winery
your glass will scarcely hold.

This legacy I freely give
of wine unorthodox
that you might be prepared to greet
your autumn equinox.

CONTENTS

INTRODUCTION

God's love for His chosen nation Israel and His church is incomprehensible. God demonstrates His love to both in the same manner; via His mercy, grace, longsuffering, favor and faithfulness.

However, while He is the awesome God of love, He is also holy, righteous, just, and perfect.

And because man is created in the image of God, man is required to emulate the attributes of his Creator.

To refuse to emulate God's attributes results in the sin of disobedience. Man has a choice.

Concerning Israel:

"See, I have set before you today life and good, death and evil, in that I command you today to love the LORD your God, to walk in His ways, and to keep His commandments...

...I call heaven and earth as witnesses today against you, that I have set before you life and death...that you may love the LORD your God, that you may obey His voice, and that you may cling to Him, for He is your life..."
Deuteronomy 30:15, 29-20 NKJV

How do the above verses affect the church?

"Now all these things happened to them as examples and they were written for our admonition, upon whom the ends of the ages have come. Therefore let him who thinks he stands take heed lest he fall."
1 Corinthians 10:11-12 NKJV

The rewards for obedience are beyond man's imagination and are eternal.

Likewise the consequences for disobedience are unfathomable and also eternal.

The ultimate obedience is to cling to the remedy for sin offered freely by the vicarious death of Christ. The ultimate disobedience is to reject that remedy.

CHAPTER 1

GOD'S LOVE FOR ISRAEL

When the majority thinks of the most significant attribute, or characteristic of God, they mostly think of His love.

There is no question about it; God definitely loves His chosen nation Israel.

Let's begin with God's covenant with Abraham, which He ratified unilaterally in approximately 2080 BC. That covenant is the foundation of the remainder of the Bible.

As history progressed, after 430 years in Egypt, God led His people out of bondage to begin the journey to the new land that He had promised them. The year was 1445 BC. And then in the 11th month of the 40th year after the Exodus, God told Moses to summarize their 40 year experience in the wilderness, just prior to their crossing the Jordan River into Canaan. The year was 1405 BC. At that time God also told Moses what Israel would think and do in the new land.

Moses' Final Words

At the time of writing the Book of Deuteronomy, the fledgling nation was well aware of their history from Genesis to the Exodus from Egypt.

Just before crossing the river, Moses told the people that what they were experiencing had never been done for any people before them. They were in fact God's chosen nation to represent Him to all the nations on the earth.

"Indeed, ask now concerning the former days which were before you, since the day that God created man on the earth, and inquire from one end of the heavens to the other. Has anything been done like this great thing, or has anything been heard like it?"
Deuteronomy 4:32 NASB

Moses reminded the people that they had heard God directly speaking to them from Mount Sinai when He proclaimed His law. The Israelites had experienced the very presence of God.

"Out of the heavens He let you hear His voice to discipline you; and on earth He let you see His great fire, and you heard His words from the midst of the fire...

...Because He loved your fathers, therefore He chose their descendants after them. And He personally brought you from Egypt by His great power..."
Deuteronomy 4:36-37 NASB

God confirmed that His mighty sovereignty and presence were given to them because He loved their ancestors. He went on to tell them that He would drive the nations out of the land which they were to inherit.

Expressions of God's Love

As we progress in presenting God's love for Israel, we'll refer to several Hebrew words and their meanings. Thereafter, when the word 'love' is used we will show which Hebrew word was the basis.

The major Hebrew word for 'love' is *ahav* with several significant synonyms including 'desire,' 'delight,' 'fond,' 'vehement,' 'affection,' 'attachment' and 'friend.'

The feminine of *ahav,* or *ahavah,* will also be used along with *chava* meaning 'cherish.' An additional Hebrew word is *chashaq* which means 'have pleasure in.' *Chashaq* expresses God's unspeakable love for His people, as well as His peoples' love for Him.

Then God made a mighty proclamation that would affect Israel and all the people on the earth from that time forward.

"So you shall keep His statutes and His commandments which I am giving you today, that it may go well with you and with your children after you..."
Deuteronomy 4:40 NASB

Moses told the people that they must cherish God's words and teach them to their children. God's word must be in their heart and in everything they say and do. They were to write God's words on their doorposts and gates. In other words, God's word was to be the most important issue in their lives.

Why Israel?

Then Moses explained to the people why God chose them and loved them.

"The LORD did not set His love (chashaq) on you nor choose you because you were more in number than any of the peoples, for you were the fewest of all peoples, but because the LORD loved (ahav) you and kept the oath which He swore to your forefathers..."
Deuteronomy 7:7-8a NASB

It is significant that God loved and chose Israel, not for any earthly or logical reason, but rather to keep His covenant He made with their father Abraham 675 years earlier. Recall, God unilaterally ratified that covenant and it is impossible for Him to lie. That is an early indication of His grace.

"And He will love (ahav) you and bless you and multiply you..."
Deuteronomy 7:13 NASB

However, the preceding verse must be considered.

"Wherefore it shall come to pass, if ye hearken to these judgments, and keep, and do them, that the LORD thy God shall keep unto thee the covenant and the mercy which he swore unto thy fathers..."
Deuteronomy 7:12 KJV

God's Love for Israel Was to be Returned

Progressing in Moses' final words to Israel, he stressed that the people must obey all of God commandments and statutes. He further told the people that they must also love the One who called them and loved them. God's love for His chosen must be reciprocated.

Then Moses detailed the blessings God would give to Israel for obedience, including their love for Him; however, we'll learn that God's love for His people will abide even though they would be disobedient. Nevertheless, there will be consequences for disobedience throughout Israel's history.

For example, Moses reminded the people of their rebellion and idolatry which required the second pair of tablets of God's laws. Israel deserved to be destroyed.

"And now, Israel, what does the LORD your God require from you, but to fear the LORD your God, to walk in all His ways and love (ahav) Him, and to serve the LORD your God with all your heart and with all your soul, and to keep the LORD's commandments and His statutes..."
Deuteronomy 10:12-13a NASB

Note again that they were to walk in **all** His ways and to love Him with their **all**.

"Yet on your fathers did the LORD set His affection to love (ahav) them, and He chose their descendants after them, even you above all peoples, as it is this day."
Deuteronomy 10:15 NASB

"You shall therefore love (ahav) the LORD your God, and always keep His charge, His statutes, His ordinances, and His commandments."
Deuteronomy 11:1 NASB

As time passed, the Israelites were disobedient and continued to stray from God's commandments. God told them if they would return to Him with repentance, He would cause them to love Him again.

"Moreover the LORD your God will circumcise your heart and the heart of your descendants, to love (ahav) the LORD your God with all your heart and with all your soul, in order that you may live."
Deuteronomy 30:6 NASB

Note the proactive actions of God that would cause the Israelites to love Him again.

And just prior to Moses' death, he summarized his words with a blessing to the children of Israel.

"Indeed, He loves (chava) the people; all Thy holy ones are in Thy hand, and they followed in Thy steps; everyone receives of Thy words."
Deuteronomy 33:3 NASB

God's Love for Israel and Israel's Love for God

Solomon in his Proverbs, and his father David along with other Psalmists, had much to say about God's love for His chosen nation, and His people's love for Him.

David loved God's temple and those who dwelt in it.

"O LORD, I love (ahav) the habitation of Thy house, and the place where Thy glory dwells"
Psalm 26:8 NASB

An unidentified Psalmist wrote extensively of Israel's awe and love for the word of God.

"Consider how I love (ahav) Your precepts...The entirety of Your word is truth, and every one of Your righteous judgments endures forever...I hate and abhor lying, but I love (ahav) Your law...Great peace have those who love (ahav) Your law..."
Psalm 119:159-160, 163, and 165 NKJV

And it is written that one should not trust in men to do what only what God can do; rather trust in the One who can do all things and loves the righteous.

"The LORD opens the eyes of the blind; the LORD raises up those who are bowed down; the LORD loves (ahav) the righteous..."
Psalm 146:8 NASB

And then Solomon, in his wisdom, summed up the truth of wisdom as it was personified as deity.

"I love (ahav) those who love (ahav) me: and those who diligently seek me will find me...From everlasting I (wisdom) was established, from the beginning, from the earliest times of the earth."
Proverbs 8:17, 23 NASB

The wisdom of God is Christ.

Solomon later proclaimed how God looks upon the wicked compared to how He looks on the righteous.

"The way of the wicked is an abomination to the LORD, but He loves (ahav) him who pursues righteousness."
Proverbs 15:9 NASB

God's Love for Israel Expressed through the Prophets

Moses died in 1405 BC. Joshua replaced him, and he died at the age of 110 in 1385 BC. That began the era of the judges which lasted until the time of the kings, which began with Saul in 1051 BC. Israel was divided into north and south in 931 BC when David's son Solomon was dethroned for his idolatry.

Even though Samuel was called a prophet, the time of the prophets typically begins with Obadiah in 850 BC.

We'll begin with prophetic words from Hosea who prophesied from 755 BC to 710 BC. It was during Hosea's time that the north was given over to Assyria in 722 BC, but that didn't affect God's love for His chosen nation.

"When Israel was a youth I loved (ahav) him, and out of Egypt I called My son...I led them with cords of a man, with bonds of love (ahavah)..."
Hosea 11:1, 4a NASB

But Israel didn't glorify God, and He responded.

"...But Assyria – he will be their king, because they refused to return to Me."
Hosea 11:5b NASB

God loved Israel from the beginning, and His love

didn't cease even though they refused to repent; rather He continued to show His love for them by chastising them.

Shortly thereafter, Hosea recorded God's invitation for Israel to repent, and He promised them that He would restore them in the latter days because of His love for them.

"O Israel, return to the LORD your God, for you have stumbled because of your iniquity...return to the LORD. Say to Him, 'Take away all iniquity; receive us graciously... Assyria shall not save us...'"
Hosea 14:1-3a NKJV

God's response:

"I will heal their backsliding, I will love (ahav) them freely, for My anger has turned away from him.'"
Hosea 14:4a NKJV

Israel is invited back; they confess that Assyria cannot save them, and then God states that He will love them freely (spontaneous, voluntary, free-will gift) and forget His anger toward them.

Isaiah Confirms God's Everlasting Love for Jacob (Israel)

Isaiah prophesied from 739 BC to 680 BC.

"But now thus says the LORD, your creator, O Jacob... For I am the LORD your God...I have given Egypt as your ransom...Since you are precious in My sight, since you are honored and I love (ahav) you..."
Isaiah 43:1, 3-4 NASB

God created Israel, and He redeemed them from Egypt; all because He loved them and would fulfill His promise to Abraham.

"For He said, 'surely, they are My people...' in His love (ahavah) and in His mercy He redeemed them; and He lifted them and carried them all the days of old. But they rebelled and grieved His Holy Spirit..."
Isaiah 63:8-10 NASB

Even in view of God's longsuffering and patience, Israel still rebelled. It becomes more obvious why God ratified His covenant with Abraham unilaterally.

Israel Will Return to God in His Time

The prophet Zephaniah, who prophesied from 635 BC to 625 BC, spoke of Judah's freedom from their Babylonian captivity as well as their status in the latter days.

"In that day it will be said to Jerusalem: 'Do not be afraid, O Zion...the LORD your God is in your midst, a victorious warrior. He will exult over you with joy, He will quiet you (silently) in His love (ahav)...'"
Zephaniah 3:16-17 NASB

Most prophecies have both a short term implication as well as a long term implication, which is usually in reference to Israel's place in the millennial kingdom.

Next we'll hear from Jeremiah who prophesied from 627 BC to 570 BC. It was during this time that Judah was sent captive to Babylon.

God has always loved Israel, and always will. Jeremiah speaks of the latter days, i.e. the millennial kingdom.

"Thus says the LORD: ... 'Yes, I have loved (ahav) you with an everlasting (eternal) love (ahavah); therefore with lovingkindness I have drawn you. Again I will build you, and you shall be rebuilt...Sing with gladness for Jacob... proclaim, give praise, and say, "O LORD, save Your people, the remnant of Israel!"""
Jeremiah 31:2-3, 7 NKJV

A new word is introduced in the above passage; it is 'remnant.' Remnant is defined in Hebrew as 'remainder,' 'residue,' 'survivors,' and 'final portion.' We'll examine that word and its significance in more detail later.

Jeremiah later reports more details of Israel's final return and restoration.

"Hear the word of the LORD, O nations, and declare in the coastlands afar off, and say, 'He who scattered Israel will gather him, and keep him as a shepherd keeps his flock.' For the LORD has ransomed Jacob, and redeemed him from the hand of him who was stronger than he."
Jeremiah 31:10-11 NASB

The short term implication is Israel's freedom from Babylonian bondage, while the long term implication is Israel's future glory in the aforementioned millennial kingdom.

God's Love for Israel Can't Be Understood with Logic

Malachi was the last of the Old Testament prophets from 437 BC to 417 BC.

Israel was questioning God's love for them because Esau was Jacob's brother. How could God love Jacob, considering Esau (Edom) was an enemy of Jacob (Israel)?

"'I have loved (ahav) you,' says the LORD. But you say, 'how hast Thou loved (ahav) us?' 'Was not Esau Jacob's brother?' declares the LORD, 'Yet I have loved (ahav) Jacob; but I have hated Esau...'"
Malachi 1:2-3 NASB

God in His longsuffering acknowledged that Esau and Jacob were brothers; however, He chose Jacob to receive Abraham's covenant. The Hebrew for 'hated' above means 'negative preference,' 'to be alienated,' or the 'desire to have no contact or relationship with another.' Thus the fact that Esau and Jacob were brothers did not mean that God looked on Esau the same way He looked on Jacob.

Therefore, while God is the sovereign Ruler of all the kingdoms on the earth, He specifically loves Jacob (Israel) and has predetermined their future position and possession, including their future King and earthly geographic boundaries.

Summary Statement

God's plan and purpose for Israel was devised from the foundation of the world.

However, through the years of Israel's history, they have been disobedient and have suffered severe consequences; nevertheless, Israel will be restored at the end of the 'Day of the LORD' and will be the seat of government during the millennial kingdom when Christ returns to rule the earth from Jerusalem.

Satan is presently the ruler of the world. As such Satan hates what God loves, and he will do his best to thwart His plans.

Consider in 2017 when President Trump declared that the United States would recognize Jerusalem as the capital of Israel.

There was an emergency meeting of the UN General Assembly to draft a resolution to negate the President's proposal.

The United Nation's vote count on that resolution to negate was 128 in favor, 9 against, and 35 abstentions, and 21 absentees.

Remember that the majority of the world's population will reject the wisdom and purpose of God.

Consider further that there are members of the United States Congress that vehemently oppose any measure or action that would benefit Israel.

Does the world not realize that Israel will always be God's chosen nation?

Most nations, including America, believe that ultimate

peace between Israel and her neighbors must focus on a two state solution, i.e. Ishmael's offspring and Isaac's offspring.

Moreover, the Bible is clear that one of the great last sins of the anti-Christ is to 'divide the land for gain.'

The final outcome is all pre-written history found in God's infallible and immutable word.

God's love for His chosen nation Israel is everlasting.

CHAPTER 2

GOD'S LOVE FOR ISRAEL WAS/IS DEMONSTRATED BY HIS MERCY, GRACE, LONGSUFFERING, FAVOR, AND FAITHFULNESS

There are two predominant Hebrew words for 'mercy.' The first is *chesedh* meaning 'compassion' 'pity,' and 'lovingkindness.' *Chesedh* presupposes the existence of a relationship between the parties involved, such as a close friend or family member. *Chesedh* is central to God's character relating to His covenant with Israel. Closely related is *chanan* witch means to 'seek' or 'implore mercy.'

Other popular Hebrew words for 'mercy' are *racham* and *rachuwm*. Both are very similar to *chesedh* with synonyms including 'cherish,' 'tenderness,' and 'love' in addition to 'compassion.'

God would be merciful by forgiving sin, but sin would have its consequences.

The People's Reluctance to Cross the River

Recall, in the second year after the Exodus, i.e. 1444 BC, when it was time to enter the Promised Land, the people refused to enter due to fear of the occupants of the land. They thought they would have been better off if they had stayed in bondage. Moses pleaded with God to forgive their sin.

"And all the sons of Israel grumbled against Moses and Aaron; and the whole congregation said to them, 'Would that we had died in the land of Egypt! Or would that we had died in this wilderness!'"
Numbers 14:2 NASB

At that point the people discussed the matter and thought it would be profitable for them to select a new leader who would take them back to bondage in Egypt.

But Joshua and Caleb stood strong and spoke to the whole congregation.

"The land we passed through to spy out is an exceedingly good land...Only do not rebel against the LORD, nor fear the people of the land...their protection has departed from them, and the LORD is with us. Do not fear them."
Numbers 14:7b, 9 NKJV

The response of the people was that they wanted to stone them.

"And the LORD said to Moses, 'How long will this people spurn Me? And how long will they not believe in Me, despite all the signs which I have performed in their midst?

I will smite them with pestilence and dispossess them, and I will make you into a nation greater and mightier than they.'"
Numbers 14:11-12 NASB

Thus God told Moses that He would disinherit the people and make him (Moses) a great nation more powerful than the people who didn't believe.

Moses Pleads for God's Mercy

One might have thought that Moses would have embraced such an offer, but instead he interceded for the people and pleaded with God to forgive them.

Moses' argument was that if God disinherited His people and the word got to Egypt and the surrounding nations, they would think that God wasn't able to deliver on His promise. Moses acknowledged Israel's sin, but asked God to forgive them.

"And now, I (Moses) pray, let the power of my Lord be great, just as You have spoken, saying, 'The LORD is longsuffering and abundant in mercy (chesedh), forgiving iniquity and transgression; but He by no means clears the guilty...Pardon the iniquity of this people, I pray according to the greatness of your mercy (chesedh) just as You have forgiven this people, from Egypt even until now.'"
Numbers 14:17-19 NKJV

God heard Moses, and said that He would pardon the people according to what Moses had said; however, He confirmed that all the people who had seen His glory, but still didn't believe, would not see the land that He had sworn to their fathers.

But Caleb, because of his faithfulness, found favor in God's sight and he and his descendants would inherit that land.

God's Mercy (Lovingkindness) Confirmed to His People Approximately 500 Years later

King Solomon spoke of God's mercy and faithfulness to keep His promises while he was praying during the dedication of the new temple.

"And he said, 'O LORD, the God of Israel, there is no God like Thee in heaven above or on earth beneath, who art keeping covenant and showing lovingkindness (chesedh) to Thy servants who walk before Thee with all their heart.'"
1 Kings 8:23 NASB

Likewise, Solomon's father David praised God for His mercy when he placed the Ark of the Covenant in the tabernacle that he had prepared in Jerusalem.

"O give thanks to the LORD, for He is good; for His lovingkindness (chesedh) is everlasting."
1 Chronicles 16:34 NASB

After the captivity in Babylon, and the remnant returned to Jerusalem with Ezra and restored the temple, the priests and Levites with trumpets sounding, sang praises to the LORD. Their song was very similar to David's praise.

"And they sang, praising and giving thanks to the LORD, saying, 'For He is good, for His lovingkindness (chesedh) is upon Israel forever.'"
Ezra 3:11a NASB

God's Mercy Proclaimed by David in His Psalms

The most oft time used phrase in the Psalms is 'God's Mercy endures Forever.'

The following is a Psalm of David as he pleads for deliverance and forgiveness.

"Remember, O LORD, Your tender mercies (racham) and Your lovingkindnesses (chesedh), for they are from old. Do not remember the sins of my youth, nor my transgressions; according to Your mercy (chesedh) remember me..."
Psalm 25:6-7 NKJV

Then David remembered God's mercy in times of adversity.

"I will be glad and rejoice in Your mercy (chesedh), for You have considered my trouble; You have known my soul in adversities...Have mercy (chanan) on me, O LORD, for I am in trouble..."
Psalm 31:7, 9 NKJV

David confirms that God's mercy will embrace those who trust in Him.

"Many are the sorrows of the wicked; but he who trusts in the LORD, lovingkindness (chesedh) shall surround him."
Psalm 32:10 NASB

David confesses his sin and prays a prayer of repentance. He pleads for God's mercy to cleanse him of his sin.

"Have mercy (chanan) upon me, O God, according to Your lovingkindness (chesedh); according to the multitude of Your tender mercies (racham), blot out my transgressions."
Psalm 51:1 NKJV

David confirms that God is merciful and impartial in rewards and chastisement.

"And lovingkindness (chesedh) is Thine, O Lord, for Thou dost recompense a man according to his work."
Psalm 62:12 NASB

Later David, while praying to God during a time of affliction, acknowledges God's lovingkindness.

"For Thou, Lord, art good, and ready to forgive, and abundant in lovingkindness (chesedh) to all who call upon Thee... Thou, O Lord, art a God merciful (rachuwm) and gracious, slow to anger and abundant in lovingkindness (chesedh) and truth."
Psalm 86:5, 15 NASB

And let's include two Proverbs by David's son Solomon which states that men should emulate God by being merciful to others.

"Let not mercy (chesedh) and truth forsake you; bind them around your neck, write them on the tablet of your heart..."
Proverbs 3:3 NKJV

Then Solomon encourages others to confess and forsake their sins and God will show compassion, i.e. mercy.

"He who conceals his transgressions will not prosper, but he who confesses and forsakes them will find compassion (racham)."
Proverbs 28:13 NASB

God's Mercy Confirmed by the Prophets

Subsequently, as God reminds Israel of their disobedience, He also confirms His eternal love for them expressed by His mercy.

The prophets mentioned will be listed in the order in which they appear in the books of the prophets and to whom they prophesied.

We'll begin with Joel who prophesied predominately to Judah from 835 BC to 796 BC.

At the time of Joel, Israel had already been divided into north (Israel) and south (Judah). The following prophecy refers to the far off future of the 'Day of the Lord' where Joel pleads for the people to return to the LORD.

"And rend your heart and not your garments. Now return to the LORD your God, for He is gracious and

compassionate (rachuwm), slow to anger, abounding in lovingkindness (chesedh)..."
Joel 2:13a NASB

Next is Hosea who prophesied to Israel from 755 BC to 710 BC.

Hosea is proclaiming God's word referencing the future millennial kingdom to be ruled by Christ after Daniel's 70th week. God will welcome back His people because He is merciful.

"I will betroth you to Me forever; yes I will betroth you to Me in righteousness and justice, in lovingkindness (chesedh) and mercy (racham)...And I will have mercy (racham) on her who had not obtained mercy (racham)..."
Hosea 2:19, 23 NKJV

And then, near the end of his prophecy, Hosea speaks of Israel's final restoration when they rely on God, and not on other nations, or their own strength. Their idols are powerless.

"Assyria will not save us, we will not ride on horses; nor will we say again, 'Our God,' to the work of our hands; for in Thee the orphan finds mercy (racham)."
Hosea 14:3 NASB

Micah prophesied to Judah from 735 BC to 710 BC and he also speaks of the final restoration of Israel during the millennial kingdom when God's mercy replaces His anger.

"Who is a God like You, pardoning iniquity and passing over the transgression of the remnant of His heritage? He

does not retain His anger forever, because He delights in mercy (chesedh)."
Micah 7:18 NKJV

The Hebrew word for 'delights' in this verse means 'to find pleasure in' and as previously stated the word 'remnant' is very significant. Recall that remnant means that only a small part of Israel will be saved, as it will be with gentiles living in the church age.

Then Micah ends his prophecy by proclaiming that God's truth and mercy for His people began in ages past and will continue to time immemorial.

"Thou wilt give truth to Jacob and unchanging love (chesedh) to Abraham, which You have sworn to our forefathers from days of old."
Micah 7:20 NASB

Note in the above that 'mercy' is expressed by 'unchanging love.'

And next is Isaiah who prophesied to Judah from 739 BC to 680 BC.

Israel, both north and south, were very stiff-necked and hesitant to break ties with enemy nations for security. However; God was longsuffering and would display His mercy in His time.

"Therefore the LORD longs to be gracious to you, and therefore He waits on high to have compassion (racham) on you. For the LORD is a God of justice; how blessed are all those who long for Him."
Isaiah 30:18 NASB

Blessings of Mercy (compassion) in Israel's Future

Subsequently God speaks of the blessings to be received with the return of the Messiah to rule the earth. His people could inherit the kingdom only by God's mercy. They will have a taste of heaven as God will lead them to 'springs of water.'

"They will not hunger or thirst, neither will the scorching heat or sun strike them down: for He who has compassion (racham) on them will lead them, and will guide them to springs of water...Shout for joy, O heavens! And rejoice, O earth...! For the LORD has comforted His people, and will have compassion (racham) on His afflicted."
Isaiah 49:10, 13 NASB

Then God confirms that His chastisement was only for a short time, but His mercy will be forever.

"For a brief moment I forsook you, but with great compassion (racham) I will gather you. In an outburst of anger I hid My face from you for a moment; but with everlasting lovingkindness (chesedh) I will have compassion (racham) on you."
Isaiah 54:7-8 NASB

And then Isaiah confirms that God's mercy will be given to those who return to Him.

"Let the wicked forsake his way, and the unrighteous man his thoughts; let him return to the LORD, and He will have mercy (racham) on him; and to our God, for He will abundantly pardon."
Isaiah 55:7 NKJV

Jeremiah Speaks of God's Mercy

Jeremiah prophesied to Judah from 627 BC to 570 BC.

Both Israel and Judah were very disobedient; however, God withheld His anger. God wanted Israel to acknowledge their sins. God would once again forsake His righteous anger for mercy.

"'Return, backsliding Israel,' says the LORD; 'I will not cause My anger to fall on you. For I am merciful (chesedh)...I will not remain angry forever. Only acknowledge your iniquity, that you have transgressed against the LORD your God..."
Jeremiah 3:12-13a NKJV

Subsequently, God confirms to Jeremiah that He will restore desolate Judah and Jerusalem with the New Covenant. They will once again rejoice because of God's mercy.

"...the voice of joy and the voice of gladness... will say: 'Praise the LORD of hosts, for the LORD is good, for His mercy (chesedh) endures forever..."
Jeremiah 33:11 NKJV

The word 'forever' is a powerful word with many synonyms including 'time immemorial' and 'without end.' Remember in the new heaven and new earth there will be no need for the sun, which is the basis for the present time dimension.

Jeremiah, as he wrote Lamentations, acknowledged that God causes grief by way of chastisement; but simultaneously exhibits compassion and mercy.

"Though He causes grief, yet He will show compassion (racham) according to the multitude of His mercies (chesedh)."
Lamentations 3:32 NKJV

Habakkuk and Daniel Proclaim God's Mercy

Habakkuk prophesied to Judah from 620 BC to 605 BC.

Habakkuk had been witnessing God's righteous chastisement on Judah's disobedience, but now he pleaded for God to redeem His chosen.

"O LORD, I have heard Your speech and was afraid; O LORD, revive Your work in the midst of the years! In the midst of the years make it known; in wrath remember mercy (racham)."
Habakkuk 3:2 NKJV

The final prophet that will be quoted is Daniel who had just returned from Babylonian captivity. He prophesied from 605 BC to 536 BC.

When Daniel realized that Judah's 70 year captivity was over, he prayed for Israel's future. Daniel was fully aware of Israel's disobedience and he knew that God's judgments were righteous. The only solution was God's mercy.

"And I prayed to the LORD my God, and made confession, and said, 'O Lord, great and awesome God, who keeps His covenant and mercy (chesedh) with those who love Him, and with those who keep His commandments...To the Lord

our God belong mercy (racham) and forgiveness, though we have rebelled against Him.'"
Daniel 9:4, 9 NKJV

The words of the prophets all confirmed that God's mercy wasn't deserved because of their disobedience; however, they knew that mercy was an attribute of their God.

God's Grace for Israel Accompanies His Mercy

There are several common Hebrew words for 'grace.'

One of the more common words for 'grace' is *chanan* with synonyms including 'kind,' 'favorable,' and 'mercy.' Another Hebrew word for 'grace' is *chen* which is a derivative of *chanan* with like synonyms including 'precious,' 'favor,' and 'kindness' while *channun* is used interchangeably with 'mercy' and 'grace.'

Recall when Joseph was in Egypt and he asked to see his youngest brother Benjamin. After much hesitation, his brothers returned with Benjamin.

"As he lifted his eyes and saw his brother Benjamin, his mother's son, he said, 'is this your youngest brother, of whom you spoke to me?' And he said, 'May God be gracious (chanan) to you my son.'"
Genesis 43:29 NASB

At that point Joseph hastily left to weep in private.

Many times it will be noted that those that taste of God's mercy, will also taste of His grace.

When God is merciful He doesn't give to His people what they deserve for their transgressions. Following mercy, God gives graciously to His people what they haven't earned or deserve.

Nehemiah Spoke of God's Grace

When Nehemiah was governor of the returned remnant of Judah in 446 BC, the repentant Levites confirmed Israel's apostasy as they read the law.

They remembered the sins of their fathers and recounted God's mercy and longsuffering in the days of Israel's redemption from Egypt a thousand years earlier.

"And they refused to listen, and did not remember Thy wondrous deeds which Thou hadst performed among them; so they became stubborn...But Thou art a God of forgiveness, gracious (channun) and compassionate (rachuwm), slow to anger, and abounding in lovingkindness (chesedh), and Thou didst not forsake them."
Nehemiah 9:17 NASB

Then after many examples of their disobedience, they said:

"Nevertheless, in Thy great compassion (racham) Thou didst not make an end of them or forsake them, for Thou art a gracious (channun) and compassionate (rachuwm) God."
Nehemiah 9:31 NASB

God's Grace in the Wisdom Books

In the Book of Psalms, the sons of Korah wrote a love song depicting the Messiah King as a groom.

"Thou art fairer than the sons of men; grace (chen) is poured upon Thy lips; therefore God has blessed Thee forever."
Psalm 45:2 NASB

The psalmist Asaph, during his younger years was troubled, but later was comforted, remembering the power and sovereignty of Almighty God.

"Has His mercy (chesedh) ceased forever? Has His promise failed forevermore? Has God forgotten to be gracious (chen)? Has He in anger shut up His tender mercies (racham)?"
Psalm 77:8-9 NKJV

"...But I will remember the years of the right hand of the Most High. I will remember the works of the LORD; surely I will remember Your wonders of old."
Psalm 77:10-11 NKJV

Then Asaph acknowledged the reality of God.

"What god is great like our God?"
Psalm 77:13b NASB

And the sons of Korah likewise acknowledged God's grace to those who were obedient, as they journeyed to Jerusalem on sacred feast days.

"For the LORD God is a sun and shield; the LORD gives grace (chen) and glory; no good thing does He withhold from those who walk uprightly."
Psalm 84:11 NASB

Solomon also spoke of those to whom God gives grace in his proverbs.

"Though He scoffs at the scoffers, yet He gives grace (chen) to the afflicted (humble)."
Proverbs 3:34 NASB

And lastly, God's word of grace is recorded by the prophet Zechariah referencing the return of the remnant to Jerusalem after the tribulation.

"And I will pour out on the house of David and on the inhabitants of Jerusalem, the Spirit of grace (chen) and of supplication, so that they will look on Me whom they have pierced; and they will mourn for Him..."
Zechariah 12:10a NASB

God Is also Longsuffering

We've noted the word 'longsuffering' in previous sections where it was used to express God's mercy.

However, the Hebrew word/words for 'longsuffering' is a combination of two words. In the current context 'long' is from the Hebrew *areph* which means 'patient,' while 'suffering' is from the Hebrew *aph* meaning 'anger' and 'wrath.' The term 'longsuffering' is frequently expressed in the Scripture as 'slow to anger' or 'patient.'

God proclaimed His longsuffering attribute when speaking to Moses when Moses ascended Mount Sinai with the two replacement tablets on which God would inscribe His commandments.

"And the LORD passed before him (Moses) and proclaimed, 'The LORD, the LORD God, merciful and gracious, longsuffering (areph/aph), and abounding in goodness and truth, keeping mercy for thousands, forgiving iniquity and transgression and sin...'"
Exodus 34:6-7 NKJV

Note in the above verse, the multiple attributes of God listed in addition to 'longsuffering,' i.e. 'merciful,' gracious,' 'goodness,' and 'truth.'

Psalms of David Referencing God's Longsuffering

David, who was king of Israel from 1011 BC to 971 BC, praised God for His longsuffering several times in the Psalms that he had written.

In the Psalm below David compares the proud, who didn't know God, to his understanding of God.

"O God, the proud have risen against me, and a mob of violent men have sought my life...but You Lord, are a God full of compassion, and gracious, longsuffering (areph/aph) and abundant in mercy and truth."
Psalm 86:14-15 NKJV

In the following Psalm, David uses the other popular term for God's longsuffering, as he also extols God's attributes of grace and mercy.

"The LORD is gracious and full of compassion, slow to anger (areph/aph) and great in mercy..."
Psalm 145:8 NKJV

The Prophets Proclaimed the Longsuffering of God

Recall Joel prophesied to Judah from 835 BC to 796 BC.

As Joel was pleading with the people to return humbly to God with repentance, he spoke of God's willingness to forgive their hard heartedness.

"...now return to the LORD your God, for He is gracious and compassionate, slow to anger (areph/aph), abounding in lovingkindness..."
Joel 2:13b NASB

Then Jonah in approximately 780 BC acknowledged God's longsuffering even though Jonah was angry with Him for His mercy to Nineveh.

"And he prayed to the LORD and said, 'Please LORD, was not this what I said while I was still in my own country? Therefore...I fled to Tarshish, for I knew that Thou are a gracious and compassionate God, slow to anger (areph/aph) and abundant in lovingkindness...'"
Jonah 4:2 NASB

Approximately 200 years later the prophet Jeremiah spoke of God's attribute of longsuffering.

As God was proclaiming the evil of His people and the consequences of their disobedience, Jeremiah pleaded for God to remember his faithfulness. Jeremiah used the synonym 'patience' in place of 'longsuffering' or 'slow to anger.'

"Thou who knowest, O LORD, remember me, take notice of me, and take vengeance for me on my persecutors. Do not, in view of Thy patience (areph/aph), take me away..."
Jeremiah 15:15 NASB

It is interesting to note that in nearly all of the above Scriptures speaking of God's longsuffering; both mercy and grace are also found in those passages.

God's Favor towards Israel

Interestingly, the Hebrew word translated 'favor' has several of the same words translated to grace, i.e. *chen* and *chanan,* but includes other Hebrew words translated 'grace' such as *ratson* meaning 'delight,' goodwill,' and 'pleasure,' and *tov* meaning 'excellent,' 'lovely,' 'fruitful,' and 'righteous.'

A very early use of *chen* for favor is found in the Book of Genesis relative to God's plan for Joseph.

"But the LORD was with Joseph and extended kindness (mercy) to him, and gave him favor (chen) in the sight of the chief jailer."
Genesis 39:21 NASB

Joseph was sent to prison for things he didn't do. It was part of God's master plan from the beginning of the world. God gave Joseph favor in the eyes of the prison guard so as to bring glory to God during his sentencing time.

However, God always has a purpose and plan. Joseph made that abundantly clear as he addressed his brothers shortly before his death.

"And as for you (brothers), you meant evil against me, but God meant it for good in order to bring about this present result, to preserve many people alive."
Genesis 50:20 NASB

Just prior to the Exodus, God gave favor to His people in the sight of the Egyptians so as to gain wealth from them with which to build the tabernacle in their near future.

"And I will grant this people favor (chen) in the sight of the Egyptians; and it shall be that when you go. You will not go empty-handed."
Exodus 3:21 NASB

"And the LORD gave the people favor (chen) in the sight of the Egyptians. Furthermore, the man Moses himself was greatly esteemed in the land of Egypt, both in the sight of Pharaohs servants and in the sight of the people."
Exodus 11:3 NASB

"...and the LORD had given the people favor (chen) in the sight of the Egyptians, so that they let them have their request. Thus they plundered the Egyptians."
Exodus 12:36 NASB

Notice how the narrative progressed from 'I will grant...' to 'the LORD gave...' to 'the LORD had given...'

Just before Moses died, he blessed the tribes of Israel as they prepared to cross over the Jordan.

His blessing to Joseph…

"...and with the choice things of the earth and its fullness, and the favor (ratson) of God who dwelt in the bush. Let it come to the head of Joseph..."
Deuteronomy 33:16 NASB

Then consider approximately 400 years later when Samuel was a young child.

"Now the boy Samuel was growing in stature and in favor (tov) both with the LORD and with men."
1 Samuel 2:26 NASB

Then 300 years after Samuel, Isaiah spoke of God's favor towards His people in the future millennial kingdom. Israel's former enemies, who God allowed to chastise them, will serve Israel's King in the future.

"The sons of foreigners shall build up your walls, and their kings shall minister to you; for in My wrath I struck you, but in My favor (ratson) I have had mercy (racham) on you."
Isaiah 60:10 NKJV

God's Favor Expressed in the Wisdom Books

Centuries later when Job was telling his friends about the gifts that God had given to him, he stated:

"You have granted me life and favor (chesedh), and Your care has preserved my spirit."
Job 10:12 NKJV

The Hebrew word *ratson* (from *ratsah*) meaning 'favor' is also the basis for 'delight' in several passages.

Subsequently Elihu was attempting to explain to Job the blessings received by a repentant man.

"He shall pray to God, and He will delight (ratson) in him, he shall see His face with joy, for He restores to man His righteousness."
Job 33:26 NKJV

In the following psalm of David, he described God's favor towards those who were righteous, and those who loved and trusted Him. Such a man should rejoice.

"...let all those rejoice who put their trust in You... let those also who love Your name be joyful in You. For You, O LORD, will bless the righteous; with favor (ratson) You will surround him as with a shield."
Psalm 5:11-12 NKJV

In another of his psalms, David spoke of the endurance of God's favor and His presence in his time of need, when David thought he was abandoned. Recall that God's anger is for the moment, His favor is forever.

"For His anger is but for a moment, His favor (ratson) is for a lifetime; weeping may last for the night, but a shout of joy comes in the morning."
Psalm 30:5 NASB

Then David realized that God had been with him all the while, and he praised Him.

An unidentified psalmist spoke of God's favor to do for Israel what they were impotent to do themselves.

"For by their own sword they did not possess the land; and their own arm did not save them; but Thy right hand, and Thine arm, and the light of Thy presence, for Thou didst favor (ratson) them."
Psalm 44:3 NASB

A prayer of the sons of Korah thanked God for the restoration of the land promised to Abraham after Judah's 70 year captivity and also looking forward to the millennial kingdom.

"O LORD, Thou didst show favor (ratson) to Thy land; Thou didst restore the captivity of Jacob."
Psalm 85:1 NASB

In another psalm the writer speaks of the glory due to God because of His favor towards Israel.

"For Thou art the glory of their strength, and by Thy favor (ratson) our horn is exalted."
Psalm 89:17 NASB

And then the Israelites recalled their weakness and implored God to deliver them from their transgressions and remember the covenant He made with Abraham.

"Remember me, O LORD, in Thy favor (ratson) toward Thy people; visit me with Thy salvation..."
Psalm 106:4 NASB

And then the psalmist speaks of God's favor towards Israel, even in times of affliction.

"You will arise and have mercy on Zion; for the time to favor (chanan) her, yes, the set time, has come."
Psalm 102:13 NKJV

It is noted that the term 'set time' is from the Hebrew *moedh* which means 'appointed.' It is the same Hebrew word used to describe the purpose of the sun in Genesis 1:14. In addition to providing light, the sun would also determine the 'seasons,' i.e. to set sacred feast days in the future.

Solomon Spoke of God's Favor to the Faithful of His People

"Do not let kindness and truth leave you; bind them around your neck write them on the tablet of your heart. So you will find favor (chen) and good repute in the sight of God and man."
Proverbs 3:3-4 NASB

"A good man will obtain favor (ratson) from the LORD, but He will condemn a man who devises evil."
Proverbs 12:2 NASB

And then Solomon personifies the supreme benefit of finding wisdom.

"For he who finds me (wisdom) finds life, and obtains favor (ratson) from the LORD."
Proverbs 8:35 NASB

Solomon also spoke of the benefit of finding a good wife. 'Good' in this context means 'excellent,' 'delightful,' 'joyful,' and 'precious,' just to name a few synonyms.

"He who finds a wife finds a good thing, and obtains favor (ratson) from the LORD."
Proverbs 18:22 NASB

God's Love for Israel Exemplified by His Faithfulness

The predominant Hebrew word translated 'faithfulness' is *emunah* derived from *aman*. Common synonyms include 'steady,' 'trust,' 'certainty,' and 'stand firm.'

During the forty years in the wilderness, Moses proclaimed to the Israelites the faithfulness of God.

"Know therefore that the LORD your God, He is God, the faithful (aman) God, who keeps His covenant and His lovingkindness to a thousandth generation with those who love Him and keep His commandments..."
Deuteronomy 7:9 NASB

God's Faithfulness in the Psalms

David oft times spoke of God's mercy and His faithfulness together.

"Your mercy, O LORD, is in the heavens; Your faithfulness (emunah) reaches to the clouds."
Psalm 36:5 NKJV

"I have spoken of Thy faithfulness (emunah) and Thy salvation; I have not concealed Thy lovingkindness and Thy truth from the great congregation. Thou, O LORD, wilt not

withhold Thy tender mercies from me; Thy lovingkindness and Thy truth will continually preserve me."
Psalm 40:10-11 NASB

In another Psalm, Ethan elaborates God's eternal faithfulness to David during trying times and in accordance with His eternal covenant.

"I will sing of the lovingkindness of the LORD forever; to all generations I will make known Thy faithfulness (emunah) with my mouth for I have said, 'Lovingkindness will be built up forever; in the heavens Thou wilt establish Thy faithfulness (emunah).'"
Psalm 89:1-2 NASB

"And the heavens will praise Thy wonders, O LORD; Thy faithfulness (emunah) also in the assembly of the holy ones."
Psalm 89:5 NASB

Then Ethan tells that God spoke in a vision to the Prophet Nathan, revealing David's future. David would be confronted by his foes...

"But My faithfulness (emunah) and My mercy shall be with him..."
Psalm 89:24 NKJV

And if David's offspring should stray, they would be punished...

"Nevertheless My lovingkindness I will not utterly take from him, nor allow My faithfulness (emunah) to fail."
Psalm 89:33 NKJV

In another psalm the unknown author praises God's love and faithfulness together continually.

"It is good to give thanks to the LORD, and to sing praises to Thy name... to declare Thy lovingkindness in the morning, and Thy faithfulness (emunah) by night..."
Psalm 92:1-2 NASB

The prophets Isaiah and Jeremiah
Spoke of God's Faithfulness

The prophet Isaiah spoke of God's faithfulness to keep His covenant from eternity past to eternity future.

"O LORD, You are my God. I will exalt You, I will praise Your name, for You have done wonderful things; Your counsels of old are faithfulness (emunah) and truth."
Isaiah 25:1 NKJV

The Hebrew word translated 'counsels' in this verse means 'purpose' and 'plan.'

And lastly, Jeremiah spoke of God's never ending mercy and faithfulness as he wrote Lamentations.

"Through the LORD's mercies (chesedh) we are not consumed, because His compassions (racham) fail not. They are new every morning; great is Your faithfulness (emunah)."
Lamentations 3:22-23 NASB

The Certainty of God's Love for Israel
Is Demonstrated through the Ages

This chapter is just a sampling of Biblical proof that God loved/loves Israel. His mercy, grace, longsuffering, favor, and faithfulness are found throughout Israel's history.

However, due to Israel's disobedience, God has now fettered their understanding.

"For the LORD has poured over you a spirit of deep sleep, He has shut your eyes, the prophets; and He has covered your heads, the seers."
Isaiah 29:10 NASB

This time of 'sleep' began during the latter time of the prophets and has continued to this day.

Is it possible that God has done that to any other nation, perhaps the nations that consider themselves to be exceptional?

Summary Statement

God's love for Israel was demonstrated by His gifts of mercy, grace, longsuffering, favor, and faithfulness throughout the Old Testament.

The fact that so many of the Old Testament books, from Genesis through Malachi, speak of God's love for Israel is major confirmation that God's word is immutable.

His love for Israel has not changed through the ages, nor will it.

God knew beforehand how Israel would respond to His love by disobeying His commandments, and the remedy for redemption; however, that wouldn't thwart His plan for His chosen nation.

Thus God placed His chosen nation in a state of stupor, beginning at the end of the prophets in the fifth century BC, in which they would not understand or comprehend His plan.

God's plan for His chosen nation will be fulfilled when the New Covenant is enacted. At that time God will indwell them with His Spirit and write His commandments on their hearts.

"...I will put My law in their minds, and write it on their hearts; and I will be their God, and they shall be My people."
Jeremiah 31:33 NKJV

Israel's best days are yet to come.

CHAPTER 3

GOD'S LOVE FOR HIS CHURCH

Thus, while Israel is sleeping, the church is flourishing. But Israel will be awakened in God's time, and will once again be the center of the world in the millennial kingdom.

Recall Paul's words relative to Israel's present status and their future.

"Again I ask: Did they stumble so as to fall beyond recovery? Not at all! Rather, because of their transgression, salvation has come to the Gentiles to make Israel envious. But if their transgression means riches for the world, and their loss means riches for the Gentiles, how much greater riches will their fullness bring!"
Romans 11:11-12 NIV

So much for supersessionism, or replacement theology.

Approximately 800 years after Isaiah foretold of Israel's stupor, Paul confirmed Isaiah's words. Israel's blindness will remain until they receive the New Covenant.

"God gave them a spirit of stupor, eyes so that they could not see and ears so that they could not hear, to this very day."
Romans 11:8 NIV

A detailed study of the phrase 'in that day' will provide much light on the future of Israel.

Love Defined in the Greek

In the New Testament there are two predominant Greek words for 'love.' The first word is *agapao*.

Agapao has a rich and multi descriptive meaning. The basis of its meaning is 'finding joy in another,' i.e. 'directing one's will.' It further means 'finding delight in another,' and 'strong affection.' *Agapao* describes God's love for man, and man's love for God.

Agapao is always used when one loves their enemies. The use of *agapao* signifies that a person desires God's very best for them including salvation.

The second major Greek word for 'love' is *phileo* meaning basically 'to be a friend,' or 'to be fond of another.' Another major aspect of the word is to 'share the same beliefs' as another and adopt their interests. Both *agapao* and *phileo* also mean 'to have a strong affection for.' As might be expected then, a person actually loves God by both *agapao* and *phileo* as does God love His people. Therefore, *agapao* and *phileo* may be used synonymously, depending on the context.

Phileo Is Experiential Love

Experiential love is known and observed by experience or examination.

"Greater love (phileo) has no one than this, that he lay down his life for his friends (philos). You are my friends (philos) if you do what I command you...I have called you friends (philos), for everything that I learned from my Father I have made known to you."
John 15:13-15 NIV

Note in the above that 'love' and 'friends' have the same Greek basis inasmuch as *phileo* is derived from *philos* and the most common synonyms for both *phileo* and *philos* is 'friend.'

Recall Jesus' friend Lazarus.

"So the sisters sent word to Jesus, 'Lord, the one you love (phileo) is sick.'"
John 11:3 NIV

The context in this verse is that Jesus and Lazarus were friends and shared common values and interests.

Subsequently, Jesus explains why the 'world' does not love the church.

"If you belonged to the world, it would love (phileo) you as its own. As it is, you do not belong to the world, but I have chosen you out of the world. That is why the world hates you."
John 15:19 NIV

The world would love the disciples if they shared the

same beliefs and interests as the world did. That is the major issue today; the division between those of the world and those of the kingdom.

Jesus proclaimed that one's love *phileo* for Him must be greater than one's love for any other.

"Anyone who loves (phileo) his father or mother more than me is not worthy of me; anyone who loves (phileo) his son or daughter more than me is not worthy of me; and anyone who does not take his cross and follow me is not worthy of me."
Matthew 10:37-38 NIV

There are times when the Father expresses His love for His Son with *phileo*.

"For the Father loves (phileo) the Son and shows him all he does."
John 5:20 NIV

Jesus told His disciples that His Father loved them because they loved Him (Jesus.)

"...the Father himself loves (phileo) you because you have loved (phileo) me and have believed that I came from God."
John 16:27 NIV

Jesus told the church at Laodicea that chastisement may be because He loved them.

"Those whom I love (phileo) I rebuke and discipline."
Revelation 3:19 NIV

And then lastly, another derivative from *phileo* is

philema meaning a token of love and friendship, i.e. 'kiss.' Note the following closing statement of Peter's first epistle.

"Greet one another with a kiss (philema) of love (phileo). 1 Peter 5:14 NIV

Other Examples of 'Love' Derived from the Greek *philos*

Christians are also to love one another, i.e. brotherly love from the Greek *philadelphia*. Appropriate synonyms include 'friendship,' 'kindness,' and 'benevolence.'

"Be devoted to one another in brotherly love (philadelphia). Honor one another above yourselves." Romans 12:10 NIV

"Now about brotherly love (philadelphia) we do not need to write to you, for you yourselves have been taught by God to love (philadelphia) each other." 1 Thessalonians 4:9 NIV

Brotherly love should be a natural thing for those who have been saved.

"Now that you have purified yourselves by obeying the truth so that you have sincere love (philadelphia) for your brothers, love (philadelphia) one another deeply, from the heart. For you have been born again..." 1 Peter 1:22 NIV

Then there is *philanthropia* which means to love mankind. This is the basis for our 'philanthropy.'

"But when the kindness and love (philanthropia) of God our Savior appeared, he saved us, not because of righteous things we had done, but because of his mercy."
Titus 3:4-5a NIV

Another word for 'love' is *philia* meaning 'friendship' and 'fondness.' In the following scripture passage, the meaning is for one to adopt the interests of the world.

"You adulterous people, don't you know that friendship (philia) with the world is hatred toward God? Anyone who chooses to be a friend (philia) of the world becomes an enemy of God."
James 4:4 NIV

Let's examine one more word for 'love' which is *philoxenia*, derived from *philos*, which means 'one who is kind to strangers,' i.e. 'hospitable.'

Paul mentioned *philoxenia* when describing the attributes of one who was saved.

"Be joyful in hope, patient in affliction, faithful in prayer. Share with God's people who are in need. Practice hospitality (philoxenia)."
Romans 12:12-13 NIV

"Keep on loving (philadelphia) each other as brothers. Do not forget to entertain (philoxenia) strangers, for by so doing some people have entertained (philoxenia) angels without knowing it."
Hebrews 13:1-2 NIV

The above is just a sampling of Scripture passages that

reference different words for 'love' from the Greek base words *philos* and *phileo*.

Differences between *Agapao*, *Agape* and *Philos*, *Phileo*

While *philos* and *phileo* are more experiential and speak mostly of love and affection between believers, *agapao* and *agape*, as previously mentioned, are more intuitive and deals more with God's love for mankind and mankind's love for God.

The final conversation that Jesus had with Peter illustrates both *agapao* and *phileo*.

"So when they had eaten breakfast, Jesus said to Simon Peter, 'Simon...do you love (agapao) Me more than these?' He (Peter) said to Him, 'Yes, Lord; You know that I love (phileo) You.'"
John 21:15 NKJV

Jesus asked Peter if he loved Him 'more than these.' There are differing thoughts on what 'more than these' means. Some think Jesus was asking Peter if he loved Him more than tangible things, i.e. Peter's fishing livelihood. While others believe Jesus was asking Peter if he loved Him more than the other disciples.

Jesus used the word *agapao* when asking Peter; Peter answered with *phileo*. Recall that *agapao* love is the highest level of love between man and God.

Peter's answer confirmed his thinking that he was a friend with Jesus, but he couldn't commit to *agapao*.

Then Jesus asked again.

"He said to him again a second time, 'Simon, son of Jonah, do you love (agapao) Me?'"
John 21:16a NKJV

Again, Jesus asked using *agapao*. The question did not contain a comparison, but an absolute, relative to Peter's love for Jesus.

"He (Peter) said to Him, 'Yes, Lord; You know that I love (phileo) (have affection for) You.'"
John 21:16b NKJV

And again, Peter responded with *phileo*, 'I am your friend.'

"He said to him the third time, 'Simon, son of Jonah, do you love (phileo) me?'"
John 21:17a NKJV

The third time Jesus asked Peter using *phileo*. He was asking Peter if he was really a friend. In other words, was Peter's perception of and loyalty to Jesus different now than before His death and resurrection? Peter would shortly be tested to see if he was really a friend to Jesus.

It was presumptuous of Peter to assume that he was a friend of Jesus at this point.

Peter's response:

"Lord, You know (intuitively) all things; You know (experientially) that I love (phileo) you."
John 21:17b NKJV

'Intuitively' means basically 'one's perception without

evidence,' or 'insight,' or 'immediate apprehension.' To 'know experientially' is from the Greek *ginosko*, which means 'to know by experience or examination.'

We'll see also that when God expresses His love for His Son He may use either, or both, *agapao* and *phileo*.

Agapao **Love Recorded in the Gospels**

Another major difference between *phileo* and *agapao* is that *agapao* recognizes the needs of others even if the others do not recognize such need. It is much more than being a friend to others, or sharing their belief system, it is intuitive. Recall that *agapao* love is the love of God toward mankind and the love that believers are commanded to have for others.

Thus *agapao* is much deeper than feelings. It also involves finding joy or delight in someone or something. *Agapao*, as well as *phileo*, will cause a person to be willing to give his life for the good of another.

Perhaps the most familiar verse in the Bible is John 3:16.

"For God so loved (agape, from agapao) the world that he gave his one and only Son, that whoever believes in him shall not perish but have eternal life."
John 3:16 NIV

The word *agape* is used in this verse because God gave man what he needed, not necessarily what he wanted, or thought he needed. God knew that man needed His Son to pay their sin debt; therefore, He gave His very best to man, whom He loved.

Following are several examples of *agapao*.

"Jesus knew that the time had come for him to leave this world and go to the Father. Having loved (agapao) his own who were in the world, he now showed them the full extent of his love (agapao)."
John 13:1 NIV

Shortly after those words, Jesus washed His disciples' feet.

And then when Judas left, Jesus went outside and spoke to His disciples.

"A new command I give you: Love (agapao) one another. As I have loved (agapao) you, so you must love (agapao) one another. By this all men will know that you are my disciples, if you love (agapao) one another."
John 13:34-35 NIV

The love that the disciples were to have for others was to be patterned after the love that Christ had for them. By doing such, all others would know the relationship between the disciples and Christ.

"As the Father has loved (agapao) me, so have I loved (agapao) you. Now remain in my love (agapao). If you obey my commands, you will remain in my love (agapao), just as I have obeyed my Father's commands and remain in his love (agapao)."
John 15:9-10 NIV

Christ again compare's His Father's love for Him with His love for His disciples. A commandment is given to illustrate how the disciples could maintain that love relationship with Christ. By keeping Jesus' commandments they could remain in His love.

"My command is this: Love (agapao) each other as I have loved (agapao) you."
John 15:12 NIV

Again, Jesus commands His disciples to love one another as He loved them. It will be quite clear that Jesus is the pattern for love between fellow men.

Jesus subsequently prayed for His disciples that they would share the same relationship with His Father as He shared.

"And I have declared to them Your name, and will declare it, that the love (agapao) with which You loved (agapao) Me may be in them, and I in them."
John 17:26 NKJV

Jesus responded to a lawyer of the Pharisees who asked which commandment was the greatest in the law.

"Jesus said to him, 'You shall love (agapao) the LORD your God with all your heart, with all your soul, and with all your mind...You shall love (agapao) your neighbor as yourself.'"
Matthew 22:37, 39 NKJV

Jesus told the Pharisees that these verses were the summation of the law.

Agapao Love in the Epistles

After Jesus' death, burial, resurrection, and ascension, Paul's teaching reinforced the words of Jesus. Whereas Jesus was teaching His disciples of the depth of God's love for Him and His disciples, Paul was teaching the church.

"For I am convinced that neither death nor life, neither angels nor demons, neither the present nor the future, nor any powers, neither height nor depth, nor anything else in all creation, will be able to separate us from the love (agapao) of God that is in Christ Jesus our Lord."
Romans 8:38-39 NIV

Paul taught that the love of God for the church enshrined in Jesus was inseparable.

God's love for His chosen was determined from the foundation of the world. He left others to their own choice and destiny.

Recall:

"Just as it is written: 'Jacob I loved (agapao), but Esau I hated.'"
Romans 9:13 NIV

The word 'hate' in this verse is the opposite of *agapao*. It means 'not to love.'

Paul told the church to be imitators of God and show love for the brethren as Christ loved them. He loved them enough to give His life for them.

"Therefore be imitators of God as dear children. And walk in love (agapao), as Christ also has loved (agapao) us and given Himself for us..."
Ephesians 5:1-2 NKJV

Subsequently in His letter to the church at Ephesus, Paul taught that the love a man has for his wife should compare to the love Christ had for the church.

"Husbands, love (agapao) your wives, just as Christ loved (agapao) the church and gave himself up for her..."
Ephesians 5:25 NIV

John also spoke of hypocrisy which occurs if one says he loves God but hates his brother.

"If anyone says, 'I love (agapao) God,' yet hates his brother, he is a liar. For anyone who does not love (agapao) his brother, whom he has seen, cannot love (agapao) God, whom he has not seen."
1 John 4:20 NIV

And then in the final Book of the Bible John introduces the letters to the churches from the Trinity.

The following describes the Son.

"...and from Jesus Christ, who is the faithful witness, the firstborn from the dead, and the ruler of the kings of the earth. To him who loves (agapao) us and has freed us from our sins by his blood..."
Revelation 1:5 NIV

This verse is in essence the description of Christ who exhibited the ultimate love for the church by cleansing His chosen from sin by paying their sin debt with His own blood.

Other Uses of *Agapao*

Not all uses of *agapao* apply to love for God or love for brothers. *Agapao* may be used to show love for tangible things, or ideology.

For example, when Jesus was denouncing the Pharisees for their hypocrisy He said:

"Woe to you Pharisees, because you love (agapao) the most important seats in the synagogues and greetings in the marketplaces."
Luke 11:43 NIV

Jesus used *agapao* when answering Nicodemus' questions relative to those who chose to reject Him and remain in sin.

"This is the verdict: Light has come into the world, but men loved (agapao) darkness instead of light because their deeds were evil."
John 3:19 NIV

Subsequently, the Apostle John warned about clinging to the world system instead of heeding the gospel.

"Do not love (agapao) the world or anything in the world. If anyone loves (agapao) the world, the love (agapao) of the Father is not in him."
1 John 2:15 NIV

And later in the Book of Revelation, John spoke of martyrs of Jesus who loved Him more than their own lives.

"They overcame him (the accuser) by the blood of the Lamb and by the word of their testimony; they did not love (agapao) their lives so much as to shrink from death."
Revelation 12:11 NIV

From *Agapao* to *Agape*

Agape is derived from *agapao*.

Agape is God's willful direction toward man. God knows what is best for man and what he needs; while man may not have the same mind and may not want what God knows is best for him.

Following are several Scripture passages written by Paul and John which speak of *agape* love.

The following is from one of Jesus' contentious conversations with pious Jews.

"...but I know you. I know that you do not have the love (agape) of God in your hearts. I have come in my Father's name, and you do not accept me..."
John 5:42 NIV

The love spoken of here should be the love that is the first priority in a man's heart.

Then consider Paul's teaching that Christ died while men still walked in sin.

"But God demonstrates his own love (agape) for us in this: While we were still sinners, Christ died for us."
Romans 5:8 NIV

The love that God has for His church is beyond comprehension.

Then John states that if love for our fellow men isn't present, then we don't know God, because love is one of God's predominant attributes.

"Whoever does not love (agape) does not know God, because God is love (agape)."
1 John 4:8 NIV

John went on to say that God demonstrated His love for His people by His actions.

"This is how God showed his love (agape) among us: He sent his one and only Son into the world that we might live through him. This is love (agape): not that we loved (agape) God, but that he loved (agape) us and sent his Son as an atoning sacrifice for our sins...Dear friends, since God so loved (agape) us, we also ought to love (agape) one another."
1 John 4:9-11a NIV

Again, God is the example of the love man should have for each other. And recall that one should be willing to give his life for a brother as Jesus did for many.

John stresses the point that God is love and that he who loves abides (remains) in love, also abides in God and God in him.

"And we have known and believed the love (agape) that God has for us. God is love (agape), and he who abides in love (agape) abides in God, and God in him."
1 John 4:16 NKJV

The Purpose of the Church

The mission of Christ and the church was established before the foundation of the world, but remained a mystery to the prophets.

"This mystery is that through the gospel the Gentiles are heirs together with Israel, members together of one body, and sharers together in the promise in Christ Jesus. I became a servant of this gospel by the gift of God's grace given me through the working of his power."
Ephesians 3:6-7 NIV

The result?

"...so that Christ may dwell in your hearts through faith. And I pray that you, being rooted and established in love (agape), may have power, together with all the saints, to grasp how wide and long and high and deep is the love (agape) of Christ, and to know this love (agape) that surpasses knowledge – that you may be filled to the measure of all the fullness of God."
Ephesians 3:17-19 NIV

Yes, God loves His church, as he loves His chosen nation, Israel.

Christ paid the sin debt for both.

Summary Statement

The first major premise in this chapter is that even though Israel is in a state of stupor, and Christ was born to establish the church, no way does that imply that the Church replaces Israel as God's favored nation.

As stated boldly at the beginning of this chapter, the concept of supersessionism was never a thought in God's plan.

The two major Greek words for 'love' are *phileo* and *agapao*.

Phileo is love generally defined as a 'friend' and 'one who shares common beliefs and has the same interests.'

Agapao is somewhat deeper, i.e. it is strong enough to direct one's will. *Agapao* expresses the love that God has for mankind and the love that mankind has for God. *Agapao* is also the expression of love that one has for their enemies. While a person may definitely not share the same interests as their enemies, each believer should desire God's best for them.

Thus, while *phileo* is experiential, *agapao* is more intuitive.

This chapter presents numerous applications of *phileo*, and its derivatives, in the gospels and epistles, as will *agapao* and its derivatives.

God's love for His Son and His people is recorded throughout the New Testament.

CHAPTER 4

GOD'S LOVE FOR HIS CHURCH IS DEMONSTRATED BY HIS MERCY, GRACE, LONGSUFFERING, FAVOR AND FAITHFULNESS

The predominant Greek word for 'mercy' is *eleeo* which is derived from *eleos*. Both words mean 'compassion,' 'pity,' and 'sympathy.' As can be seen *eleeo* is very similar in meaning to the Hebrew *chesedh* which means 'mercy' as previously stated.

This chapter will confirm that the church will receive the same love from God as did His chosen nation Israel.

The first Scripture verses in this chapter will focus on God's mercy for His church.

Christians were taught that just as God is merciful towards men, men were told to emulate God's mercy when dealing with fellow Christians.

The premise of emulating God's attributes and characteristics will be discussed in detail in chapter 6.

God's Mercy Expressed in the Epistles

In Paul's letter to the Christians in Rome He stressed that God will choose to whom He will give mercy.

A great truth is that not all men will receive God's mercy, but all will experience His righteousness and justice.

"For he says to Moses, 'I will have mercy (eleeo) on whom I have mercy (eleeo), and I will have compassion on whom I have compassion.' It does not, therefore, depend on man's desire or effort but on God's mercy (eleeo)."
Romans 9:15-16 NIV

Paul is saying that neither human effort nor human choice have anything to do with obtaining God's mercy.

In his greeting to the church in Corinth, Paul confirmed that God was the source and giver of mercy.

"Blessed be the God and Father of our Lord Jesus Christ, the Father of mercies (eleeo) and God of all comfort who comforts us in all our tribulation, that we may be able to comfort those who are in any trouble, with the comfort which we ourselves are comforted by God."
2 Corinthians 1:3-4 NKJV

Peter, in his first letter to dispersed Christians and Jews in what is now modern Turkey, spoke of God's mercy in bringing His own to salvation.

"Praise be to the God and Father of our Lord Jesus Christ! In his great mercy (eleeo) he has given us new birth into a living hope through the resurrection of Jesus

Christ from the dead, and into an inheritance that can never perish, spoil or fade – kept in heaven for you..."
1 Peter 1:3-4 NIV

Note that mercy was given because of God's great love for His people.

Subsequently, Paul wrote to his friend and protégé Titus and spoke of God's love for those created in His image, and His mercy to give life.

"But when the kindness and love of God our Savior appeared, he saved us, not because of righteous things we had done, but because of his mercy (eleeo)."
Titus 3:4-5a NIV

The theme remains the same, i.e. man is saved by God's mercy, and salvation has nothing to do with man's performance.

And then just prior to his death, Paul wrote to his disciple and friend Timothy and spoke of God's mercy.

"Even though I was once a blasphemer and a persecutor and a violent man, I was shown mercy (eleeo) because I acted in ignorance and unbelief."
1Timothy 1:13 NIV

God overlooked Paul's wretched past and transformed him into a faithful servant.

Paul boldly told Timothy that the only reason for his position with God was because of God's mercy. Paul deserved nothing.

God's Grace Follows His Mercy

Recall that God's mercy saves us from what we deserve, while His grace provides us with that which we do not deserve.

The predominant Greek word for 'grace' in the New Testament is *charis* which means in essence a 'free gift.' Grace reflects favor and goodwill given by God and Christ to men. Grace demonstrates God's favor given without expecting a return.

Several other significant synonyms for 'grace' include 'favor,' 'benefit,' 'forgiveness,' 'acceptance,' and 'freedom.'

Charis is from the Greek *chairo* meaning 'to rejoice' and 'be glad for the grace given.' Additional synonyms include 'to cheer,' 'celebrate,' and 'to make merry.'

Grace is found in the New Testament Scriptures from the gospels, through the epistles, and is mentioned in the final verse in the Bible.

Recall when Jesus and His parents returned to Galilee from Egypt after Herod died in 4 BC.

"And the child grew and became strong; he was filled with wisdom, and the grace (charis) of God was upon him." Luke 2:40 NIV

While the Father's grace was upon His Son in His early years, the Son would become the giver of grace in His adult years.

John announced the incarnation of Jesus and described

Him as the Son of God, possessing attributes of deity, including grace.

"The Word became flesh and made his dwelling among us. We have seen his glory, the glory of the One and Only, who came from the Father, full of grace (charis) and truth."
John 1:14 NIV

Shortly thereafter John compared the law with grace. Recall, no man could obey the law in full.

"From the fullness of his grace (charis) we have all received one blessing after another. For the law was given through Moses; grace (charis) and truth came through Jesus Christ."
John 1:16-17 NIV

These verses introduce the truth that salvation was only possible because of God's grace, i.e. the gift of the life of His Son to pay man's sin debt.

God's Grace Expressed in the Epistles

Then after the death, burial, resurrection, and ascension of Jesus, the apostles taught the gospel message of salvation by grace alone to the fledgling church.

When Peter spoke at the Jerusalem Council he stated that Gentiles could be saved in the same manner as Jews.

"We believe it is through the grace (charis) of our Lord Jesus that we are saved, just as they are."
Acts 15:11 NIV

Subsequently as Paul was considering the persecutions

and tribulations awaiting him as he traveled to Jerusalem, he proclaimed:

"However, I consider my life worth nothing to me, if only I may finish the race and complete the task the Lord Jesus has given me – the task of testifying to the gospel of God's grace (charis)."
Acts 20:24 NIV

Paul was reaffirming the words of John and Peter, i.e. the gospel message focused on salvation by grace, and not by attempting to obey the law. Paul was also giving the priority of sharing that message by facing his trials and tribulations with confidence knowing he was fulfilling God's will for him.

Paul's basic message was salvation by faith in Jesus Christ apart from the law. Faith is also a gift of grace from God.

"...for all have sinned and fall short of the glory of God, and are justified freely by his grace (charis) through the redemption that came by Christ Jesus."
Romans 3:23-24 NIV

Then Paul compared the death of Adam and the accompanying consequences with the life given freely through Christ.

"...For if the many died by the trespass of the one man, how much more did God's grace (charis) and the gift that came by the grace (charis) of the one man, Jesus Christ, overflow to the many!"
Romans 5:15 NIV

Then Paul summarized his argument by proclaiming that the purpose of the law was to define sin.

"The law was added so that the trespass might increase. But where sin increased, grace (charis) increased all the more, so that, just as sin reigned in death, so also grace (charis) might reign through righteousness to bring eternal life through Jesus Christ our Lord."
Romans 5:20-21 NIV

The more sin abounded, the more grace abounded to conquer the consequences of breaking the law. Grace provided salvation by the death of Christ which fulfilled the law, which no man could do.

Paul then confirmed that the saved remnant of Israel was due to God's grace, and not by the works of the law.

"So too, at the present time there is a remnant chosen by grace (charis). And if by grace (charis), then it is no longer by works; if it were, grace (charis) would no longer be grace (charis)."
Romans 11:5-6 NIV

Recall, a remnant is defined as the small part remaining after the whole has been dealt with. The remnant was elected by God's grace. Again, the saved remnant had nothing to do with man's attempt to obey the law.

In Paul's greeting to the church in Corinth, he proclaimed that everything they had was due to God's grace.

"I always thank God for you because of his grace (charis) given you in Christ Jesus. For in him you have been enriched in every way..."
1 Corinthians 1:4-5a NIV

In that same letter Paul told the church at Corinth that due to God's grace, he (Paul) laid the foundation for that church, i.e. preached the gospel of Jesus Christ for the members to build on and grow.

"By the grace (charis) God has given me, I laid a foundation as an expert builder, and someone else is building on it."
1 Corinthians 3:10 NIV

Then Paul recounts what he was before God's grace, and states that His grace was not given in vain, inasmuch as he labored all the more with the power of God's grace.

"But by the grace (charis) of God I am what I am, and his grace (charis) to me was not without effect. No, I worked harder than all of them – yet not I, but the grace (charis) of God that was with me."
1 Corinthians 15:10 NIV

In his second letter to the church in Corinth, Paul was telling of the thorn in his flesh which was given to him to prevent him from being proud.

"Three times I pleaded with the Lord to take it away from me. But he said to me, 'My grace (charis) is sufficient for you for my power is made perfect in weakness.'"
2 Corinthians 12:8-9 NIV

God was saying that Paul needed nothing more than His grace, and He would be glorified in Paul's weakness.

In his letter to the church in Ephesus Paul speaks of God's grace given to His chosen, though His Son, from the foundation of the world. The unspeakable result is that His chosen ones are now adopted sons of the Father and joint heirs with Jesus.

"For he chose us in Him before the creation of the world to be holy and blameless in his sight. In love He predestined us to be adopted as his sons through Jesus Christ, in accordance with his pleasure and will – to the praise of his glorious grace (charis), which he has freely given us in the One he loves."
Ephesians 1:4-6 NIV

Paul continued to confirm that redemption and forgiveness were also due to God's grace.

"In him we have redemption through his blood, the forgiveness of sins, in accordance with the riches of God's grace (charis) ..."
Ephesians 1:7 NIV

One of the greatest Scripture passages on grace is found later in the same letter where Paul speaks of God's multiple attributes of love, mercy, and grace.

"But because of his great love for us, God, who is rich in mercy, made us alive with Christ even when we were dead in transgressions – it is by grace (charis) you have been saved."
Ephesians 2:4-5 NIV

It all began with God's love for His people who were spiritually dead because of sin, but He gave life through His grace to be in the presence of His Son.

Paul continues to tell of the eternal future of those recipients of God's grace, all because of the gift of His Son.

"And God raised us up with Christ and seated us with him in the heavenly realms in Christ Jesus, in order that in the coming ages he might show the incomparable riches of his grace (charis)...for it is by grace (charis) you have been saved, through faith – and this not from yourselves, it is the gift of God..."
Ephesians 2:6-8 NIV

In Paul's second letter to the church in Thessalonica He states that God's grace is eternal and covers everything in the life of His people.

"May our Lord Jesus Christ himself and God our Father, who loved us and by his grace (charis) gave us eternal encouragement and good hope, encourage your hearts and strengthen you in every good deed and word."
2 Thessalonians 2:16-17 NIV

And once again, Paul confirms to Titus that man was totally impotent to save himself. Salvation was only possible by the mercy and grace of the Almighty.

"...He saved us through the washing of rebirth and renewal by the Holy Spirit, whom he poured out on us generously through Jesus Christ our Savior, so that, having

been justified by his grace (charis), we might become heirs having the hope of eternal life."
Titus 3:5b-7 NIV

God's grace justified sinful men, resulting in newness of life and becoming joint heirs with Jesus Christ throughout eternity.

The apostle Peter confirms that the grace of God is a gift to His chosen, and the recipients of His grace should be stewards of that gift.

"Each one should use whatever gift he has received to serve others, faithfully administering God's grace (charis) in its various forms."
1 Peter 4:10 NIV

And finally, John while on the Island of Patmos, closes the Bible with the admonition that the grace of Jesus be received by all who read and abide by His final teachings and warnings.

"The grace (charis) of the Lord Jesus be with God's people. Amen"
Revelation 22:21 NIV

God Is Longsuffering towards His Church

There are several Greek words translated 'longsuffering' including *hupomone* with several popular synonyms including 'forbearance' and 'patience.' Another Greek word for 'longsuffering' is *makrothumia* also meaning 'forbearance' plus 'restraint.' And then there is *anoche* which includes the meaning of 'temporary longsuffering.'

One of the most significant aspects of God's longsuffering is His forbearance of sin's consequence immediately, but giving time for the sinner to repent.

Paul made it well known to practicing sinners that they should change their ways before their judgment. He told them they should not test God on His patience with them.

"Or do you despise the riches of His goodness, forbearance, and longsuffering (makrothumia), not knowing that the goodness of God leads you to repentance?"
Romans 2:4 NKJV

Paul subsequently taught the significance of the cross. His teaching emphasized that Christ's death paid for the sins committed previously by those who came to faith in Christ's vicarious death.

"...whom God set forth as a propitiation by His blood, through faith, to demonstrate His righteousness, because in His forbearance (anoche) God had passed over the sins that were previously committed..."
Romans 3:25 NKJV

When Jews questioned God's justice and His sovereignty, Paul responded by stating that God had the power to give mercy to whom He chose and let the unrepentant reap God's wrath. Then Paul gave an example.

"What if God, wanting to show His wrath and to make His power known, endured with much longsuffering (makrothumia) the vessels of wrath prepared for destruction..."
Romans 9:22 NKJV

God has the power and the right to punish sin in His time to fulfill His purpose. Those choosing not to repent prepared themselves for destruction.

And in Paul's benediction in his second letter to the church at Thessalonica he reminded the members of God's patience.

"Now may the Lord direct your hearts into the love of God and into the patience (hupomone) of Christ."
2 Thessalonians 3:5 NKJV

God's Favor towards His Church

There are far fewer times in the New Testament where the words 'favor' and 'faithfulness' are found compared to 'mercy' and 'grace.'

A primary reason is that the most used Greek word for 'favor' is the feminine noun *charis*, i.e. the same Greek word translated for 'grace.' *Charis* is also the primary Greek word translated 'acceptance.' Therefore, 'grace,' 'favor,' and 'acceptance' could be found being used interchangeably.

For example:

Recall the words that the angel Gabriel spoke to Mary when he announced that Mary would be the mother of the Son of God.

"The angel went to her and said, 'Greetings, you who are highly favored (charis)! The Lord is with you...Do not be afraid, Mary, you have found favor (charis) with God.'"
Luke 1:28, 30 NIV

The message would have the same significance if either 'grace' or 'acceptance' would have been used in place of 'favor.'

A similar example is found in the second chapter of Luke while Jesus was still a young man.

"And Jesus grew in wisdom and stature, and in favor (charis) with God and men."
Luke 2:52 NIV

Subsequent to Jesus' death, burial, resurrection, and ascension, Stephen was called a blasphemer by Jewish leaders when he boldly spoke of the history of the Jews and the role of Jesus.

Several of his points included God's favor to historical chosen ones.

One of those who found favor in God's eyes was Jacob's son Joseph when he was sold as a slave in Egypt and imprisoned for things he didn't do.

"And the patriarchs, becoming envious, sold Joseph into Egypt. But God was with him and delivered him out of all his troubles, and gave him favor (charis) and wisdom in the presence of Pharaoh..."
Acts 7:10 NKJV

Stephen continued his dissertation of Israel's history chronologically up to the time of David. Recall the tabernacle remained in the desert...

"...until the time of David, who enjoyed God's favor (charis)..."
Acts 7:45b-46a NIV

And once again, these passages would not have lost meaning if either of the words 'grace' or 'acceptance' had been used instead of 'favor.'

God's Faithfulness for His Chosen Ones

Two primary Greek words translated 'faithfulness' are *elpis* and *pistos*. *Elpis* represents 'hope with expectation,' while *pistos* means 'worthy of belief,' 'trust,' or 'confidence.'

Paul, Peter, John, and the writer of Hebrews spoke of God's faithfulness using the Greek *pistos*.

Synonyms for 'faithfulness' translated from the Greek *pistos* also include 'unmovable,' 'steadfast,' 'irrevocable,' and 'truthful.'

In his first letter to the church at Corinth, Paul spoke of God's faithfulness in calling His chosen ones to salvation and completing the work that He began in them.

"God, who has called you into fellowship with his Son Jesus Christ our Lord, is faithful (pistos)."
1 Corinthians 1:9 NIV

In his first letter to the church at Thessalonica, Paul confirmed the profound truth of God fulfilling His calling of His chosen and preserving them for the return of His Son.

"The one who calls you is faithful (pistos) and he will do it."
1 Thessalonians 5:24 NIV

In his second letter to the church at Thessalonica Paul was warning his brothers to beware of wicked men who attempted to distort the truth by spewing deceitful teachings.

"But the Lord is faithful (pistos), and he will strengthen and protect you from the evil one."
2 Thessalonians 3:3 NIV

The writer of Hebrews tells that Jesus had to be in the form of His brothers in order to be a faithful High Priest and be the sin offering for them.

"For this reason he had to made like his brothers in every way in order that he might become a merciful and faithful (pistos) high priest in service to God, and that he might make atonement for the sins of the people."
Hebrews 2:17 NIV

Shortly thereafter, the same writer confirmed that the promises by God to His people were irrevocable.

"Let us hold unswervingly to the hope we profess, for he who promised is faithful (pistos)."
Hebrews 10:23 NIV

Peter, while teaching about rejoicing during suffering, referenced God as a faithful Creator.

And those who have the gift of suffering for the sake of Christ should be even more committed to God's will and word.

"So then, those who suffer according to God's will should commit themselves to their faithful (pistos) Creator and continue to do good."
1 Peter 4:19 NIV

And then John taught about God's faithfulness in forgiving sin upon confession.

"If we confess our sins, he is faithful (pistos) and just and will forgive us our sins and purify us from all unrighteousness."
1 John 1:9 NIV

Summary Statement

Up to this point, we have referenced the Bible to prove in detail the extent of God's love for His chosen nation Israel under the Old Covenant, and His love for His church under the New Covenant.

The New Covenant will be revealed to Israel at the end of the 'day of the LORD' when God's Spirit indwells Israel's remnant, such as the church presently enjoys.

This chapter detailed numerous examples presented in the gospels and epistles explaining God's love for His church by His mercy, grace, longsuffering, favor, and faithfulness, i.e. in the same manner that He demonstrated His love for His chosen nation Israel.

Most of His people see Him only as the God of love, but…

CHAPTER 5

GOD IS ALSO HOLY, RIGHTEOUS, JUST, AND PERFECT

The preceding chapters proclaimed that God is love, confirmed by His plan and patience toward His chosen nation Israel, as well as His New Testament church.

And while most tend to focus on God's attribute of love, He is so much more than that as evidenced by this chapter's title.

God's Holiness Revealed to Israel

In the Old Testament, the primary Hebrew word for 'holy' is *qadhash*. Primary synonyms for *qadhash* include 'sanctify,' 'hallow,' 'dedicate,' 'consecrate,' and 'purify.' When other Hebrew words are used for 'holy' such as *qadhosh*, they are predominantly from the root *qadhash*.

The Bible provides numerous examples of holiness for God the Father, God the Son, and God the Holy Spirit.

When Pharaoh and his army pursued the Israelites

fleeing from bondage to freedom, God caused His people to cross over the Red Sea on dry land, and then let the waters return to destroy those who sought to destroy His people.

Thus Israel saw the great work which the LORD had done to Pharaoh and his army, and they feared the LORD and believed Him and his servant Moses.

As they celebrated their freedom, the people and Moses sang a song to the LORD.

"Who is like unto thee, O LORD, among the gods? Who is like thee, glorious in holiness (qodhesh), fearful in praises, doing wonders?"
Exodus 15:11 KJV

Moses contends that God's glorious holiness surpasses anything attributed to pagan gods.

Approximately 400 years later Samuel's mother Hannah acknowledged the supremacy of God's holiness.

"There is none holy (qadhosh) like the LORD; for there is none beside thee, neither is there any rock like our God."
1 Samuel 2:2 KJV

Subsequently, King David acknowledged God's holiness in his Psalms. The short term application was for David during a time of trial, while the Psalm ultimately applied to the future Messiah.

"My God, my God, why hast thou forsaken me?...O my God, I cry in the daytime, but thou hearest not...but thou

are holy (qadhosh), O thou who inhabitest the praises of Israel....

...our fathers trusted in Thee: they trusted, and thou didst deliver them."
Psalm 22:1a-4 KJV

God's Holiness Referenced in the Prophecy of Isaiah

But 300 years after David, things had changed.

Recall when the prophet Isaiah denounced Israel's sins and disobedience in the beginning of his prophetic book.

"Ah, sinful nation, a people laden with iniquity...children that are corrupters...

"...they have forsaken the LORD, they have provoked the Holy (qadhosh) One of Israel unto anger, they are gone away backward."
Isaiah 1:4 KJV

Isaiah uses the phrase 'the Holy One of Israel' more than two dozen times in his prophecies.

Subsequently, Isaiah tells of the judgment of God for Israel's disobedience.

"But the LORD of hosts shall be exalted in justice, and God, who is holy (qadhosh), shall be sanctified in righteousness."
Isaiah 5:16 KJV

God's judgment is righteous and He will be lifted up and hallowed for doing what is just.

In a vision, Isaiah saw the Lord sitting upon a throne and seraphim standing above the throne of God proclaiming His holiness.

"And one cried unto another, and said, Holy (qadhosh), holy (qadhosh), holy (qadhosh), is the LORD of hosts; the whole earth is full of his glory."
Isaiah 6:3 KJV

That was a precursor for what John would see when he was taken up to heaven for a vision of Daniel's 70th week.

Then God spoke to Isaiah reminding Israel who He is.

"Thus saith the LORD, your Redeemer, the Holy (qadhosh) One of Israel...I am the LORD, your Holy (qadhosh) One, the creator of Israel, your King."
Isaiah 43:14a, 15 KJV

"For thus saith the high and lofty One who inhabiteth eternity, whose name is Holy (qadhosh): I dwell in the high and holy (qadhosh) place, with him also who is of a contrite and humble spirit..."
Isaiah 57:15a KJV

God is the Holy One above all else, and He dwells in His holy place. He will revive and restore those who are contrite and humble to dwell with Him.

God also spoke of the holiness of His Son, the Messiah, to come.

"Thus saith the LORD, the Redeemer of Israel, and his Holy (qadhosh) One, to him whom man despiseth, to him whom the nation abhorreth, to a servant of rulers: Kings

shall see and arise, princes also shall worship, because of the LORD who is faithful, and the Holy (qadhosh) One of Israel, and he shall choose thee."
Isaiah 49:7 KJV

Even though the coming Messiah is the Holy One of Israel, the Son of the Almighty, he would be despised and rejected. However, at the end of the 'Day of the Lord,' the despised One will rule all nations and kings with a rod of iron.

The Holiness of God Revealed in the Gospels

Recall, the holiness of God is attributed to God the Father, God the Son, and God the Holy Spirit.

A common Greek adjective for 'holy' is *hagios*, meaning 'pious,' 'pure,' and 'without spot.'

Matthew describes the parents of the Messiah. His mother was with child before she and her betrothed husband had been together: a miracle of the Almighty.

"Now the birth of Jesus Christ was as follows: After His mother Mary was betrothed to Joseph, before they came together, she was found with child of the Holy (hagios) Spirit."
Matthew 1:18 NKJV

God the Son was conceived by God the Holy Spirit at the direction of God the Father. The Spirit of God is always referred to as the Holy Spirit.

Luke also addressed the conversation that Gabriel had with Mary.

"The angel answered, 'The Holy (hagios) Spirit will come upon you, and the power of the Most High will overshadow you. So the holy (hagios) one to be born will be called the Son of God.'"
Luke 1:35 NIV

This verse speaks both of the Holy Spirit and the Holy One to be born, which is God the Son.

Recall, the prophet Isaiah spoke of the coming Messiah as 'their (Israel's) Holy One.'

Shortly thereafter, Mary visited Elizabeth and spoke of the greatness and holiness of God who had chosen her and gave life to the One in her womb.

"...for the Mighty One has done great things for me – holy (hagios) is his name."
Luke 1:49 NIV

The Holy One of Israel as an Adult in the Gospels

As Jesus began His ministry, Luke told the story of Jesus casting a demon out of a man. The demon cried out to Jesus saying:

"What do you want with us, Jesus of Nazareth? Have you come to destroy us? I know who you are – the Holy (hagios) One of God!"
Luke 4:34 NIV

And then the Holy One of God cast the demon out of the man, to the amazement of all who witnessed the miracle.

Jesus always acknowledged the holiness of His Father.

As Jesus was approaching the time of His departure, He prayed for His disciples and those who would hear the gospel message from them.

"I will remain in the world no longer, but they are still in the world, and I am coming to you. Holy (hagios) Father, protect them by the power of your name – the name you gave me – so that they may be one as we are one."
John 17:11 NIV

It is so amazing that the Son of God actually prayed for us.

Jesus, the Holy One in the Epistles

After Jesus' death, burial, resurrection and ascension, the church was founded. The apostle Peter quoted David in reference to Jesus as the Holy One while recounting the history of Jesus and the significance of His crucifixion.

"For You will not leave my soul in Hades, nor will You allow Your Holy (hagios) One to see corruption."
Acts 2:27 NKJV

Synonyms for 'corruption' in this verse include 'destruction' and 'grave.'

Then Peter told the Jews that they had denied the Messiah, just as Isaiah had prophesied.

"You disowned the Holy (hagios) and Righteous One and asked that a murderer be released to you. You killed the author of life..."
Acts 3:14-15a NIV

Shortly thereafter, Stephen delivered a detailed account of the history of Jesus and referred to the holiness of the third person of the Godhead, i.e. the Holy Spirit, while referring to Jesus, as the Righteous (Just) One.

"You stiff-necked people, with uncircumcised hearts and ears! You are just like your fathers: You always resist the Holy (hagios) Spirit! Was there ever a prophet your fathers did not persecute? They even killed those who predicted the coming of the Righteous (Just) One."
Acts 7:51-52 NIV

The writer of Hebrews subsequently spoke of Christ as being the holy High Priest forever, according to the order of Melchizedek.

"Such a high priest meets our need – one who is holy (hagios), blameless, pure, set apart from sinner, exalted above the heavens."
Hebrews 7:26 NIV

And then moving on to the first epistle of John, he tells new Christians that they have an anointing from Jesus, the Holy One.

"But you (little children) have an anointing from the Holy (hagios) One, and all of you know the truth."
1 John 2:20 NIV

The Apostle John Sees the Holy One
in the Book of Revelation

Subsequently John, in the Spirit, finds himself experiencing the future. He beheld the throne of the Almighty and heard the four living creatures speaking as referenced by Isaiah 800 years earlier.

"Holy (hagios), holy (hagios), holy (hagios) is the Lord God Almighty, who was, and is, and is to come."
Revelation 4:8b NIV

Then just prior to the final seven bowl judgments, John heard seven angels singing the song of Moses and the song of the Lamb.

"Who will not fear you, O Lord, and bring glory to your name? For you alone are holy (hosios). All nations will come and worship before you, for your righteous acts have been revealed."
Revelation 15:4 NIV

The Greek adjective *hosios* is used in this Scripture passage which speaks of God as the pre-eminent Holy One.

Holiness Ascribed to other than Deity

God teaches His people that His priests shall be holy and His people should obey His (God's) words, and therefore practice holiness.

"Thou shalt sanctify him therefore; for he offereth the bread of thy God; he shall be holy (qadhosh) unto thee; for I, the LORD who sanctifieth you, am holy (qadhosh)."
Leviticus 21:8 KJV

In Peter's second epistle, he affirmed that holy men of God were inspired by the Holy Spirit of God.

"...for prophecy never came by the will of man, but holy (hagios) men of God spoke as they were moved by the Holy (hagios) Spirit."
2 Peter 1:21 NKJV

And in the last chapter of the Bible, God's prophets are called holy as well as New Jerusalem.

"Then he (one of the seven angels) said to me (John), 'These words are faithful and true.' And the Lord God of the holy (hagios) prophets sent His angel to show His servants the things which must shortly take place."
Revelation 22:6 NKJV

"...and if anyone takes away from the words of the book of this prophecy, God shall take away his part from the Book of Life, from the holy (hagios) city, and the things which are written in this book."
Revelation 22:18 NKJV

God's Righteousness and Justice Revealed to His Chosen Nation Israel

The primary Hebrew word for 'righteousness' is the noun *tsedheq*. The verb and adjective forms of this word are very similar to the noun; thus we'll not distinguish their differences when used in Old Testament verses.

Tsedheq has several meanings. The primary synonym is 'justice,' thus 'righteousness' and 'justice' can be used interchangeably.

Other synonyms for *tsedheq* include 'integrity,' 'fair,' 'honest,' and 'equity.' The phrase 'not partial' is found several times in the place of 'equity.'

However, another Hebrew word for 'justice,' 'judge,' and 'judgment' is the verb *shaphat* which means 'to rule' and 'give justice.' Also there is the noun *mishpat* (from *shaphat*) translated 'judgment' with synonyms meaning 'verdict,' 'due,' 'right,' and 'law.'

When righteous and justice are used in the context of government, they apply to all three functions, i.e. legislative, judicial, and executive.

Recall when Isaiah spoke of the reign of Christ when He returns to rule from Jerusalem.

"But there the majestic LORD will be for us... for the LORD is our Judge, the LORD is our Lawgiver, the LORD is our King."
Isaiah 33:21a, 22a NKJV

There are also Scripture passages that state that God is 'without transgressions,' 'without sin,' 'without iniquity,' or is 'not unjust.' Such phrases define 'righteousness.'

We'll site many examples of God's righteousness and justice in the Old Testament.

For example:

Just prior to entering the Promised Land, Moses spoke to the assembly of Israelites about administering justice in the land they were about to possess.

"Judges (shaphat) and officers shalt thou make thee in all thy gates...and they shall judge (shaphat) the people with just (tsedheq) judgment (mishpat). Thou shalt not distort justice (mishpat)."
Deuteronomy 16:18 KJV

God's Righteousness Proclaimed
by Ezra and Nehemiah

Approximately a millennium after the events in Deuteronomy, Ezra returned to Judah from Persia to rebuild the temple in Jerusalem that had been destroyed just prior to their Babylonian captivity. He found many examples of disobedience of God's people after their return from Babylon. When discussing the intermarriage between Israelites and pagans, he extolled God's righteousness.

"O LORD God of Israel, You are righteous (tsaddiq) for we are left as a remnant, as it is this day."
Ezra 9:15 NKJV

The Hebrew adjective *tsaddiq* is found in this verse which is derived from the verb *tsadheq*, as is *tsedheq*.

Recall later when Nehemiah was the governor of Jerusalem he led the third group of returnees from Babylon in approximately 445 BC. Nehemiah's mission was to rebuild the walls of the city.

Similar to Ezra, the Israelites owned up to their disobedience and God was 'just' to chastise them.

"Howbeit, thou art just (tsaddiq) in all that is brought upon us; for thou hast done right, but we have done wickedly..."
Nehemiah 9:33 KJV

The Righteousness of God in the Psalms

Perhaps the Book of the Old Testament that contains the most references to God's righteousness is the Book of Psalms, particularly Psalms of David.

"The fear of the LORD is clean, enduring forever; the judgments (mishpat) of the LORD are true and righteous (tsadheq) altogether."
Psalm 19:9 NKJV

In this Psalm David is extolling the attributes of God Almighty, including His righteousness *tsadheq* in all things.

The following is a verse from a Psalm written by Asaph which also declares the righteousness of God.

"And the heavens shall declare his righteousness (tsedheq); for God is judge (shaphat) himself. Selah."
Psalm 50:6 KJV

Following is another Psalm by Asaph as he pleads for God's justice.

"God standeth in the congregation of the mighty; he judgeth (shaphat) among the gods...defend the poor and fatherless: do justice (tsedheq) to the afflicted and needy."
Psalm 82:1, 3 KJV

Another unidentified Psalmist also spoke of God's attributes of justice and judgment to guide them.

"Justice (tsedheq) and judgment (mishpat) are the habitation of thy throne: mercy and truth shall go before thy face."
Psalm 89:14 KJV

God made it perfectly clear who He was and what He stood for.

Another Psalmist tells of the eternal aspect of God's righteousness.

"His work is honorable and glorious, and His righteousness (tsedheq) endureth forever."
Psalm 111:3 KJV

God's righteousness will never change.

And then another unnamed Psalmist tells of God delivering him from death. Note also that three of God's attributes are mentioned in this verse, i.e. grace, righteousness, and mercy.

"Gracious is the LORD, and righteous (tsaddiq); yes, our God is merciful."
Psalm 116:5 KJV

In the following Psalm, the writer is acknowledging the righteous judgments of God.

"Righteous (tsaddiq) art thou, O LORD, and upright are thy judgments. Thy testimonies, that thou hast commanded, are righteous (tsedheq) and very faithful."
Psalm 119:137-138 KJV

Man should attempt to live according to God's commandments, inasmuch as His commandments are righteous and just.

In another Psalm of David, he proclaims that God is righteous and gracious in everything.

"The LORD is righteous (tsaddiq) in all His ways, gracious in all His works."
Psalm 145:17 NKJV

Let's look at one of Solomon's Proverbs which speaks of God's blessings for the man who is just.

"The curse of the LORD is in the house of the wicked; but he blesseth the habitation of the just (tsaddiq)."
Proverbs 3:33 KJV

God Speaks of His Righteousness through His Prophets

God invites Israel to determine if there is anyone or any idol that can do what He does.

"Tell ye, and bring them near; yea, let them take counsel together. Who hath declared this from ancient time?...Have not I, the LORD? And there is no God else beside me, a just (tsaddiq) God and Savior; there is none beside me."
Isaiah 45:21 KJV

No one or anything can compare to the sovereignty and majesty of the Almighty.

Then Jeremiah quotes God's word that any and all glory belongs to Him alone.

"'...Let not the wise man glory in his wisdom... but let him that glorieth glory in this, that he understandeth and knoweth me, that I am the LORD who exerciseth loving-kindness, justice (mishpat), and righteousness (tsedhaqah), in the earth; for in these things I delight,' saith the LORD."
Jeremiah 9:23-24 KJV

What a basic but profound lesson; a man should not glory in himself, but his glory should always be directed to the only One who deserves glory, i.e. the sovereign God.

Then Ezekiel speaks of the attributes of the righteous man.

"...if a man be just (tsaddiq), and do that which is lawful and right (tsedhaqah)...hath executed true judgment (mishpat) between man and man, hath walked in my statutes, and hath kept my judgments (mishpat), to deal truly; he is just (tsaddiq), he shall surely live..."
Ezekiel 18:5, 8b-9 KJV

Ezekiel subsequently speaks of the laws applicable to the Prince during the future millennial temple.

"Thus saith the Lord God...remove violence and spoil, and execute judgment (mishpat) and justice (tsedhaqah)..."
Ezekiel 45:9 KJV

The prophet Micah tells of God's plea for Israel to repent and return to Him.

"He hath showed thee, O man, what is good; and what doth the LORD require of thee, but to do justly (mishpat), and to love mercy and walk humbly with thy God?"
Micah 6:8 KJV

Then the prophet Zephaniah speaks of God's righteousness in the midst of Jerusalem's wickedness.

"The just (tsaddiq) LORD is in the midst thereof; he will not do iniquity: every morning doth he bring his judgment (mishpat) to light, he faileth not; but the unjust knoweth no shame."
Zephaniah 3:5 KJV

To summarize this section, the writer of the following Psalm warns all mankind that God will judge the world, with His righteousness being the benchmark.

"...for he cometh to judge (tsedheq) the earth; he shall judge (tsedheq) the world with righteousness (tsedheq), and the people with his truth."
Psalm 96:13 KJV

The world had best take God at His word.

God's Righteousness Described in the New Testament

The primary Greek word for 'righteousness' is *dikaios* along with other similar words derived from *dikaios* depending on whether the meaning is a noun, verb, or adjective.

And again, the primary synonym for 'righteousness' is 'just.'

We'll examine several New Testament Scripture passages describing God's righteousness from the gospels, epistles, and the final Book in the Bible.

Recall when Jesus prayed for us prior to His crucifixion.

"Righteous (dikaios) Father, though the world does not know you, I know you, and they know that you have sent me."
John 17:25 NIV

Jesus addresses His Father as righteous. We'll see shortly that Jesus Himself is referred to as righteous.

Subsequently, Paul addressed the men of Athens and spoke of the righteousness of God. God has not judged sin previously committed because of lack of knowledge, giving sinners a chance to repent before His righteous judgment.

"In the past God overlooked such ignorance, but now he commands all people everywhere to repent. For he has set a day when he will judge the world with justice (dikaios) by the man he has appointed."
Acts 17:30-31a NIV

God requires men to acknowledge and espouse His righteousness and repent, or face the judgment day when Christ will judge the world justly.

Paul later spoke of God's righteousness to the believers in Rome.

"I am not ashamed of the gospel...for in the gospel a righteousness (dikaios) from God is revealed, a righteousness (dikaios) that is by faith..."
Romans 1:16a-17a NIV

Shortly thereafter, Paul spoke of the ignorance of Israel by seeking their own righteousness. Paul prayed for them to know the truth. Their zeal was misdirected.

"Since they did not know the righteousness (dikaios) that comes from God and sought to establish their own, they did not submit to God's righteousness (dikaios). Christ is the end of the law so that there may be righteousness (dikaios) for everyone who believes."
Romans 10:3-4 NIV

Paul's sorrow for Israel was that they were seeking to please God with their own righteousness by attempting to obey the law. No one can obey the law fully; the only remedy is for sinless Christ to fulfill the law on their behalf.

Therefore, faith produces righteousness, and faith is also a gift of God.

"Therefore no one will be declared righteous in his sight by observing the law; rather, through the law we become conscious of sin. But now a righteousness (dikaios) from God, apart from law, has been made known...This righteousness (dikaios) from God comes through faith in Jesus Christ to all who believe."
Romans 3:20-22 NIV

Paul subsequently explained in more detail the fact that Christ went to the cross to pay man's sin debt.

"God presented him (Jesus) as a sacrifice of atonement, through faith in his blood. He did this to demonstrate his justice (dikaios)..."
Romans 3:25a NIV

God demonstrated His justice (righteousness) by sending His Son to the cross to show that all sin must be paid for.

And then Peter confirmed the teaching of Paul.

Peter addressed the suffering of Christ, and how He humbly did His Father's will.

"When they hurled their insults at him, he did not retaliate; when he suffered, he made no threats. Instead, he entrusted himself to him who judges justly (dikaios). He himself bore our sins in his body on the tree, so that we might die to sins and live for righteousness (dikaios)..."
1 Peter 2:23-24 NIV

God's Righteousness in the Book of Revelation

Then in the final Book of the Bible, John speaks of God's righteousness.

Just before the seven angels poured out the seven last plagues, they spoke of God's attributes of truth and justice.

"...Great and marvelous are your deeds, Lord God Almighty. Just (dikaios) and true are your ways, king of the ages!"
Revelation 15:3b NIV

And while John was in heaven in the spirit, he heard an angel speak as rivers and springs of water became blood.

"...You are righteous (dikaios), O Lord, the One who is and who was and who is to be, because You have judged these things."
Revelation 16:5 NKJV

The angel went on to say that those that shed the blood of God's people were given blood to drink, and such was their 'just' due.

Then as the third bowl is poured out, another angel proclaimed:

"Yes, Lord God Almighty, true and just (dikaios) are your judgments."
Revelation 16:7b NIV

And then as mighty Babylon falls, John heard a multitude singing.

"Hallelujah! Salvation and glory and power belong to our God, for true and just (dikaios) are his judgments. He has condemned the great prostitute who corrupted the earth by her adulteries."
Revelation 19:1b-2a NIV

The Righteousness of God the Son (the Just One)

Recall the main synonym for 'righteousness' in the Greek is 'just.'

When Jesus had breathed His last, a centurion had witnessed Jesus' time on the cross. The centurion knew Christ was innocent of all charges.

"The centurion, seeing what had happened, praised God and said, 'Surely this was a righteous (dikaios) man.'"
Luke 23:47 NIV

Of course He was a righteous man, He was God.

In the following verse John also refers to Christ as the Righteous One.

"...But if anybody does sin, we have one who speaks to the Father in our defense – Jesus Christ, the Righteous (dikaios) One."
1 John 2:1b NIV

And recall when Peter was speaking to the people about Jesus and referred to Him as the Holy One and the Just.

"The God of Abraham, Isaac and Jacob, the God of our fathers, has glorified his servant Jesus. You handed him over to be killed...You disowned the Holy and Righteous (dikaios) One..."
Acts 3:13-14a NIV

And then Stephen gave a burning indictment to the Jews for killing Jesus. Stephen presented the history of the Messiah from the time of Abraham.

"Was there ever a prophet your fathers did not persecute? They even killed those who predicted the coming of the Righteous (dikaios) One. And now you have betrayed and murdered him..."
Acts 7:52 NIV

Stephen was stoned to death for telling the truth.

Paul later addressed a crowd in Jerusalem and told them

about His conversion and the words that God's servant Ananias spoke to him. Paul was told by Ananias that he would know the Messiah.

"Then he said: 'The God of our fathers has chosen you to know his will and to see the Righteous (dikaios) One and to hear words from his mouth.'"
Acts 22:14 NIV

In Peter's first letter to dispersed Christians, he spoke of the suffering of the righteous One for the benefit of the unrighteous.

"For Christ died for sins once for all, the righteous (dikaios) for the unrighteous, to bring you to God."
1 Peter 3:18a NIV

Peter was saying that Christ, the Just One, died for unjust sinners.

Later John reaffirmed that same message in his first epistle.

"If we confess our sins, He is faithful and just (dikaios) and will forgive us our sins and purify us from all unrighteousness."
1 John 1:9 NIV

God is Perfect

The major Hebrew word for 'perfect' is the adjective *tamim* with major synonyms including 'complete,' 'whole,' and 'upright.' Other words which may be translated from *tamim* include 'faultless,' 'innocent,' and 'blameless.'

Recall when God admonished Abram to be perfect, or in the following verse 'blameless.'

"And when Abram was ninety years old and nine, the LORD appeared to Abram, and said unto him, 'I am the Almighty God; walk before me, and be thou 'perfect (tamim).'"
Genesis 17:1 KJV

Thus Abram was to receive the immutable covenant that would affect all mankind through the ages. And note that God admonished Abram to be perfect also. Man is to emulate God's attributes.

Then 675 years later Moses would proclaim the perfection of God to the Israelites just prior to their crossing the Jordan River.

"Because I will proclaim the name of the LORD; ascribe ye greatness unto our God. He is the Rock, his work is perfect (tamim); for all his ways are justice (mishpat); a God of truth and without iniquity, just (tsaddiq) and right is he."
Deuteronomy 32:3-4 KJV

Notice the accompanying descriptive words of God's attributes in addition to 'perfect,' i.e. 'justice,' 'truth,' 'without iniquity,' 'just and right.' Whenever a single attribute is ascribed to God, nearly always other attributes are included.

Let's go forward another 400 years to the time of David. David ascribed greatness to His God when he was delivered from the hands of Saul.

"As for God, his way is perfect (tamim); the word of the LORD is tried: he is a shield to all them that trust in him... God is my strength and power; and he maketh my way perfect (tamim).
2 Samuel 22:31, 33 KJV

David acknowledged that not only was God perfect, but God would make him (David) perfect.

Satan Was once Perfect?

Satan was in fact perfect before he fell from glory.

Then 400 years after the reign of Kind David, the prophet Ezekiel proclaimed God's words describing Satan's glory prior to his pride.

"You were the anointed cherub...I established you...you were perfect (tamim) in your ways from the day you were created, till iniquity was found in you."
Ezekiel 28:14-15 NKJV

Note a major part of Satan's iniquity as he manipulated the King of Tyre.

"By the multitude of thy merchandise...Thou hast defiled thy sanctuaries by the iniquity of thy merchandise..."
Ezekiel 28:16a, 18a KJV

Is that relevant to current priorities in America?

God's Perfection in the New Testament

The primary Greek word for 'perfect' is *telos*, from which we get *teleios*, from which we get *teleioo*.

Telos primarily means 'completion,' 'end,' and 'termination.' *Teleios* is similar, meaning 'finished,' 'goal,' and 'that which has reached its end.'

Teleioo follows with a similar meaning 'to complete and made perfect by reaching its intended goal.'

John's gospel message described wonderfully and powerfully the major meaning and result of Christ's vicarious death on the cross.

"Later, knowing that all was now completed (teleioo), and so that the Scripture would be fulfilled, Jesus said, 'I am thirsty...' When he had received the drink, Jesus said, 'It is finished (teleioo). With that, he bowed his head and gave up his spirit."
John 19:28, 30 NIV

Subsequently the writer of Hebrews summarized Jesus' mission and His accomplishment ordained by His Father from the foundation of the world.

"In bringing many sons to glory, it was fitting that God...should make the author of their salvation perfect (teleioo) through suffering."
Hebrews 2:10 NIV

The writer then confirmed the glorious blessings of Jesus' sacrifice.

"Although he was a son, he learned obedience from what he suffered and, once made perfect (teleioo), he became the source of eternal salvation for all who obey him."
Hebrews 5:8-9 NIV

Jesus is the eternal High Priest.

"Such a high priest meets our need...Unlike the other high priests, he does not need to offer sacrifices day after day, first for his own sins, and then for the sins of the people...For the law appoints as high priests men who are weak; but the oath, which came after the law, appointed the Son, who has been made perfect (teleioo) forever."
Hebrews 7:26-28 NIV

As Jesus is, so should be His people.

"Therefore we also...let us run with endurance the race that is set before us, looking unto Jesus, the author and finisher (perfecter, i.e. teleiotes) of our faith, who for the joy that was set before Him endured the cross..."
Hebrews 12:1-2a NKJV

The work that God has begun in His people will be fulfilled by the time that Christ returns for His church. Paul said it succinctly in his letter to the church in Philippi.

"I thank my God every time I remember you...being confident of this, that he who began a good work in you will carry it on to completion (perfection), i.e., (teleioo) until the day of Christ Jesus."
Philippians 1:3a, 6 NIV

Praise God for His unspeakable plan for His people devised from the foundation of the world!

Summary Statement

God's attributes describe His innate character.

God's attributes are absolute, immutable, and everlasting.

Thus, God's attributes also define mankind's divine standard of living. His attributes were introduced to Israel and, therefore, are defined plentifully throughout the Old Testament. Numerous relative Scripture passages are presented from the Pentateuch, through the historical books, the wisdom books, and numerous prophets.

God's immutable attributes are also confirmed and illustrated throughout the gospels, epistles, and in the Book of Revelation.

The majority tends to focus on God's mercy and love, with less thought given to His holiness, righteousness, and justice. However, not all will taste of God's mercy, but all will taste of His justice.

CHAPTER 6

EMULATING THE ATTRIBUTES OF GOD

One of the most significant truths in the Bible, as it relates to God's requirement for man's obedience, is for God's people to emulate His attributes.

Why is that truth so foundational?

That question can be answered by referring to the sixth day of creation.

"Then God said, 'Let Us make man in Our image, according to Our likeness; and let them rule over the fish of the sea and over the birds of the sky and over the cattle and over all the earth,'...and God created man in His own image, in the image of God He created him; male and female He created them."
Genesis 1:26-27 NASB

Therefore, inasmuch as man was created in the image of God, and believers are joint heirs with His begotten Son, it confirms that God is working in believers to transform them into the image of His Son, i.e. God in the flesh.

It is significant that God the Son did not take on the

form of angels, but rather the Seed of Abraham. Recall that God the Son is the Seed of the woman in Genesis 3:15.

This truth is found in many Scriptures. For Example in Paul's letter to the church at Philippi, he taught that Christ 'emptied Himself' and forsook His privileges of deity to take on the form of His brothers in the flesh.

"...Christ Jesus, who, being in the form of God, did not consider it robbery (harpagmos) to be equal with God, but made Himself of no reputation, taking the form of a bondservant, and coming in the likeness of men... He humbled Himself and became obedient to the point of death, even the death of the cross."
Philippians 2:5b-8 NKJV

The Greek word for 'robbery,' in the present context is *harpagmos* which means 'to seize,' or 'something to hold on to.'

The writer of the book of Hebrews offers more explanation of the necessity of the incarnation of Christ in the flesh.

"For verily he took not on him the nature of angels, but he took on him the seed of Abraham. Wherefore, in all things it behooved him to be made like his brethren, that he might be a merciful and faithful high priest in things pertaining to God, to make reconciliation for the sins of the people."
Hebrews 2:16-17 KJV

It was necessary for the high priest of the people to be as one like them.

"For we have not an high priest who cannot be touched with the feeling of our infirmities, but was in all points tempted like as we are, yet without sin."
Hebrews 2:18 KJV

Thus Paul in his letter to the church in Galatia describes the results of Christ having been in the likeness of men.

"I have been crucified with Christ; it is no longer I who live, but Christ lives in me; and the life which I now live in the flesh I live by faith in the Son of God, who loved me and gave Himself for me."
Galatians 2:20 NKJV

And in his letter to the church at Philippi, Paul expounded on that teaching.

"...according to my earnest expectation and hope that in nothing I shall be ashamed, but with all boldness, as always, so now also Christ will be magnified in my body, whether by life or by death."
Philippians 1:20 NKJV

To make that point we'll examine several attributes of God and see what the Bible says about man's duty to emulate them. We'll begin by discussing the major attributes of love, holiness, righteousness, justness, and perfection.

Then in the latter part of this chapter we'll discuss the attributes of God by which He showed His love for His people, i.e. mercy, grace, longsuffering, and faithfulness.

"Therefore be imitators (walk in) of God, as beloved children, and walk in love (agapao), just as Christ also loved (agapao) you, and gave Himself up for us..."
Ephesians 5:1-2 NASB

Firstly, God Commands Man to Love Him and also his Fellowman

"And you shall love (ahav) the LORD your God with all your heart and with all your soul and with all your might..."
Deuteronomy 6:5 NASB

The Hebrew word for 'love' in the above passage, i.e. *ahav* means 'delight,' 'desire,' 'affection,' and 'to take pleasure in.'

To love 'the LORD your God' is found numerous times in both the Old and New Testament.

When the Israelites had taken possession of the land and just prior to Joshua's death, he told the people of God's command to love Him and keep His commandments.

"But take careful heed to do the commandment and the law which Moses....commanded you, to love the LORD your God, to walk in all His ways, to keep His commandments, to hold fast to Him, and to serve Him with all your heart and with all your soul."
Joshua 22:5 NKJV

And recall that God told Moses to tell the people that they were also to love others as their selves.

"You shall not hate your fellow-countryman in your heart...You shall not take vengeance... but you shall love (ahav) your neighbor as yourself; I am the LORD...You are to keep (shamar) My statutes."
Leviticus 19:17a, 18-19a NASB

Loving God and Others during and after the Time of Christ

Jesus taught that one should also love *(agape)* his enemies. He taught that there is no reward for loving one who loves you.

"You have heard it said, 'You shall love your neighbor and hate your enemy.' But I say to you, love your enemies bless those who curse you, do good to those who hate you..."
Matthew 5:43-44 NKJV

Just before Jesus' departure, He gave a new commandment to His disciples.

"A new commandment I give to you that you love one another; as I have loved you...By this all will know that you are My disciples, if you have love for one another."
John 13:34-35 NKJV

Paul teaches that of all the gifts of the Spirit, the greatest gift is to have love. Any good deeds if not given in love are meaningless.

"Love never faileth...and now abideth faith, hope, love, these three; but the greatest of these is love."
1 Corinthians 13:8a, 13 KJV

Paul offers more details, i.e. love is longsuffering, is kind, is not envious, is not arrogant, is not rude, is not provoked, thinks no evil, does not rejoice in one's troubles, rejoices in truth, bears all things, believes all things, hopes all things, endure all things.

After reminding the people of the commandments to follow Paul states the following:

"...all are summed up in this saying, namely, 'You shall love your neighbor as yourself.' Love does no harm to a neighbor; therefore love is the fulfillment of the law."
Romans 13:9b-10 NKJV

In his letter to the church at Colosse Paul taught that the elect of God are holy and beloved. Then he tells of things that a believer should espouse such as mercy, meekness, and longsuffering.

"But above all these things put on love, which is the bond of perfection."
Colossians 3:14 NKJV

Then John tells us that God isn't expecting His people to do something that He wouldn't do. When we love God, it is simply returning the love He first had for us. Throughout the entire Scriptures, God never commands us to do anything that He hasn't already done for us.

"We love Him because He first loved us."
1 John 4:19 NKJV

Then John tells us to love one another in the same manner that He has already loved us.

"Beloved, if God so loved us, we also ought to love one another."
1 John 4:11 NASB

God Commands Man to be Holy

God's people were to be holy both as a nation and as individuals.

Recall 'holy' in the Hebrew means 'sacred' or 'consecrated.'

God told Israel that if they would obey His commandments, they would be a special nation above all others.

"...and you shall be to Me a kingdom of priests and a holy nation."
Exodus 19:6 NASB

When God was providing detailed instructions to Moses relative to ceremonial laws, He added that the Israelites should imitate His holiness.

"For I am the LORD, who brought you up from the land of Egypt, to be your God; thus you shall be holy for I am holy."
Leviticus 11:45 NASB

Then as God was speaking to Moses about moral laws and warning of things of which they should not participate...

"And you shall be holy to Me, for I the LORD am holy, and have separated you from the peoples, that you should be Mine."
Leviticus 20:26 NKJV

And then 700 years later, Isaiah was speaking of Israel's people in their capital city in the millennial kingdom.

"And they will call them, 'The holy people, the redeemed of the LORD...'"
Isaiah 62:12 NASB

Emulating God's Holiness in the Church Age

During the church age the apostles spoke of the holiness of God's people. The Greek meaning of 'holy' is similar to the Hebrew, i.e. 'pure' and 'sacred.'

Paul in his letter to the church in Ephesus was speaking of God's unspeakable blessings to His people.

"...just as He chose us in Him before the foundation of the world, that we should be holy and blameless before Him..."
Ephesians 1:4 NASB

In this same letter Paul tells that those elected believers have been given the innate attribute of holiness and righteousness.

"...and be renewed in the spirit of your mind, and that you put on the new man which was created according to God, in true righteousness and holiness."
Ephesians 4:23b-24 NKJV

Paul reiterated that truth in his second letter to the church at Corinth.

"Therefore, having these promises beloved, let us cleanse ourselves from all filthiness of the flesh and spirit, perfecting holiness in the fear of God."
2 Corinthians 7:1 NKJV

The writer of Hebrews states that if others can't see holiness in a person, they may miss seeing the LORD in that person and thus may not recognize God's invitation to salvation.

"Pursue peace with all people, and holiness, without which no one will see the Lord: looking carefully lest anyone fall short of the grace of God..."
Hebrews 12:14 NKJV

And lastly Peter taught that holiness must be an integral part of a believer's life if he is to live as an obedient child of God. Recall a previous Scripture quoted from Peter:

"...but as He who called you is holy, you also be holy in all our conduct, because it is written, 'Be holy, for I am holy.'"
1 Peter 1:15 NKJV

God Commands Man to be Righteous and Just

The following passage not only speaks of man's righteousness, but also of the significance of obedience, which will be the focal point of the following chapters.

Obedience to God's commandments will be righteousness for the believer.

"And the LORD commanded us to observe (shamar) all these statutes...then it will be righteousness (tsedheq) for us, if we are careful to observe (shamar) all these commandments before the LORD our God...."
Deuteronomy 6:24-25 NKJV

Note again that God commands man to observe **all** His commandments and statutes. Obedience produces righteousness.

"The LORD opens the eyes of the blind; the LORD raises up those who are bowed down; the LORD loves the righteous (tsaddiq)."
Psalm 146:8 NASB

Recall, the Hebrew word 'righteous' in this verse has several significant synonyms including 'honest,' and 'just.' Righteousness is obedience to the law as stated above in the passage from Deuteronomy.

The word 'just' meaning 'righteousness,' is found in Isaiah.

"The way of the just (tsaddiq) is uprightness; O Most Upright, You weigh the path of the just (tsaddiq)."
Isaiah 26:7 NKJV

Notice that the Hebrew word for 'just' in the above is *tsaddiq* which is the same Hebrew word for the 'righteous' in the preceding psalm.

The prophet Micah records God's plea for Israel to return to Him. He reminds them what He did to idolatrous nations so that His people will be aware of His righteousness.

"O My people, remember now (what I did to) Balak... that you may know the righteousness of the LORD. He has shown you, O man, what is good; and what does the LORD require of you but to do justly..."
Micah 6:5a, 8 NKJV

Righteousness Taught by Jesus

Early in His ministry Jesus taught the significance of righteousness.

Recall the beatitudes which He taught in His Sermon on the Mount.

"Blessed are those who hunger and thirst for righteousness, for they shall be filled."
Matthew 5:6 NKJV

The word 'hunger' in this verse is from the Greek *peinao* meaning metaphorically 'to long for something other than literal food.'

The word 'thirst' is from the Greek *dipsao* meaning 'to desire ardently.' We'll expound on this word and meaning in the final chapter of this book.

Shortly thereafter, Jesus taught the priority of seeking righteousness relative to other things needed for daily living.

"But seek first the kingdom of God and His righteousness, and all these things shall be added to you."
Matthew 6:33 NKJV

The Greek word for 'righteousness' in the above verses

is *dikaiosune,* which means 'acceptance' and 'conformity' to all of God's standards. And *dikaiosune* also means 'just' as in the Hebrew.

And as mentioned under the attribute of holiness, that same verse stated that the believer was created both in righteousness and holiness.

Righteousness Taught in the Epistles

In Paul's letter to the Christians in Rome, he taught that righteousness in the church was comparable with God's work with David in his Psalm 32, written a millennium earlier.

The point that Paul was making was that righteousness can be imputed to one who doesn't depend on his works to be justified.

"...just as David also describes the blessedness of the man to whom God imputes righteousness apart from the law: 'Blessed are those whose lawless deeds are forgiven...'"
Romans 4:6-7 NKJV

In his second letter to the church in Corinth, Paul described the vicarious death of Christ as the way to reconciliation with God.

"For He made Him who knew no sin to be sin for us, that we might become the righteousness of God in Him."
2 Corinthians 5:21 NKJV

In his letter to the church at Ephesus, Paul taught that righteousness is an innate attribute of God's chosen.

"...and that you be renewed in the spirit of your mind, and put on the new self, which in the likeness of God has been created in righteousness and holiness of the truth."
Ephesians 4:23-24 NASB

Subsequently, Paul prayed for the Philippians, for their spiritual growth and understanding of their righteousness given by Christ.

"And this I pray, that your love may abound still more and more in knowledge and all discernment...being filled with the fruits of righteousness which are by Jesus Christ..."
Philippians 1:9, 11 NKJV

Paul subsequently confirmed the impotence of his own righteousness, and the truth of the effectiveness of the righteousness of Christ paying his sin debt on the cross. Anything other than the cross was considered rubbish by Paul.

"...that I may gain Christ and be found in Him, not having my own righteousness, which is from the law, but that which is through faith in Christ, the righteousness which is from God by faith..."
Philippians 3:8b-9 NKJV

In the wonderful chapter on faith in the Book of Hebrews, the writer tells of righteousness granted to those of faith.

"By faith Noah, being divinely warned of things not yet seen...prepared an ark...and became heir of the righteousness which is according to faith."
Hebrews 11:7 NKJV

The writer later tells that God's chastening ends in righteousness.

"Now no chastening seems to be joyful for the present, but painful; nevertheless, afterward it yields the peaceable fruit of righteousness to those who have been trained by it."
Hebrews 12:11 NKJV

Then James quotes Genesis 15:6 where God grants righteousness to Abraham because he took God at His word. This verse is so significant that it is quoted numerous times in the New Testament.

"And the Scripture was fulfilled which says, 'Abraham believed God, and it was accounted to him for righteousness.' And he was called the friend of God."
James 2:23 NKJV

James also stressed that genuine faith is proven by one's actions.

And lastly, John tells that he who believes in God's righteousness and anxiously awaits the return of Christ has been born again and practices righteousness until Christ's return.

"If you know that He is righteous, you know that everyone who practices righteousness is born of Him."
1 John 2:29 NKJV

God Commands Man to be Perfect

As previously mentioned, 'perfection' in the Greek is *telos* from which we get *teleios* and has several significant synonyms including 'complete,' 'end,' 'finish,' and 'to reach the end goal.'

In His early teachings Jesus was expounding on the importance of loving one's neighbor. He proclaimed that His Father was perfect and that should be the aspiration of the believer. And that is only possible by the vicarious death of Christ.

"Therefore you are to be perfect (teleios), as your heavenly Father is perfect (teleios)."
Matthew 5:48 NASB

Paul taught that believers have been given gifts for the edifying of the church till…

"…we all come to the unity of the faith and of the knowledge of the Son of God, to a perfect (teleios) man, to the measure of the stature of the fullness (teleios) of Christ."
Ephesians 4:13 NKJV

Note that the same Greek word, i.e. *teleios*, is used translated to both 'perfect' and 'fullness.'

In Paul's letter to the church at Colosse he was telling of the mystery of the church, until Christ founded it.

"Him we preach, warning every man and teaching every man in all wisdom that we may present every man perfect (teleios) in Christ Jesus."
Colossians 1:28 NKJV

Recall that *teleios* from *telos* means to 'reach the end goal.'

Near the end of that letter, Paul proclaimed that a

bondservant of Christ named Epaphras was praying for the Colossians to attain the goal of perfection and completion of God's will for them.

"...always laboring fervently for you in prayers, that you may stand perfect (telios) and complete (teleios) in all the will of God."
Colossians 4:12 NKJV

God Commands His People to be Merciful

In a previous section relative to God requiring His people to pursue righteousness and justice, that same verse from Micah also stated that His people should love mercy.

"He has shown you, O man, what is good; and what does the LORD require of you but to do justly, and love mercy (chesedh)..."
Micah 6:8 NKJV

Recall that *chesedh* means 'kindness,' or 'lovingkindness.'

In the prophecy of Hosea, God condemns Israel for their indifference.

"Hear the word of the LORD, you children of Israel... there is no truth or mercy (chesedh) or knowledge of God in the land."
Hosea 4:1 NKJV

Thus, not to show mercy was a sin.

Solomon told of the advantages of showing mercy to the poor and needy. God honors the merciful.

"He who oppresses the poor reproaches His Maker, but he who honors Him has mercy on the needy."
Proverbs 14:31 NKJV

God Commands His People to be Merciful in the New Testament

Mercy likewise begins with the beatitudes given by Jesus in His Sermon on the Mount.

"Blessed are the merciful, for they shall obtain mercy."
Matthew 5:7 NKJV

Luke records a discussion that Jesus had with a lawyer who asked Jesus what he should do to inherit eternal life. Jesus in turn asked what the scriptures said, and the lawyer correctly answered that one must love God with his all, and love his neighbor as himself.

Jesus confirmed that the lawyer answered correctly. Then the lawyer asked who his neighbor was.

Jesus then told the parable of the Good Samaritan. The parable was about a certain man who fell among thieves and was left for dead. A priest, a Levite, and a Samaritan saw the man. The priest and Levite passed by, but the Samaritan stopped and cared for the man.

And while the priest and the Levite were pious Jews, Samaritans were not held in favor by the Jews due to their assimilating into the culture of the Assyrians when the northern ten tribes were overtaken by Assyria seven centuries earlier.

Jesus asked the lawyer which man was the neighbor.

"And he said, 'He who showed mercy on him.' Then Jesus said to him, 'Go and do likewise.'"
Luke 10:37 NKJV

In his letter to the Christians in Rome, Paul spoke of gifts that God had given graciously to His people. His people are to use their gifts productively to the glory of the giver.

At the end of the listing of numerous gifts, Paul said:

"...he who gives, with liberality; he who leads, with diligence; he who shows mercy, with cheerfulness."
Romans 12:8 NKJV

Thus, mercy is a gift given to God's people for His glory.

God Commands His People to be Gracious

In his letter to the church at Ephesus, Paul said that he was given grace so that he could be a more effective man of God.

"To me, who am less than the least of all the saints, this grace was given, that I should preach among the Gentiles the unsearchable riches of Christ..."
Ephesus 3:8 NKJV

Recall that 'grace' is from the Greek *charis* meaning primarily a 'gift.'

In the benediction of that letter Paul implored that peace, love, faith, and grace be given to all believers so as to edify the church.

"Peace to the brethren, and love with faith, from God...
Grace be with all those who love our Lord Jesus Christ in
sincerity."
Ephesians 6:23-24 NKJV

Subsequently, the writer of the Book of Hebrews also asked for God's grace which would be used to more effectively serve the giver of grace.

"Therefore, since we are receiving a kingdom which
cannot be shaken, let us have grace, by which we may serve
God acceptably with reverence and godly fear."
Hebrews 12:28 NKJV

Peter closes his second letter with similar instructions; use the grace given by God to grow and thus be a more effective servant. He warns God's people to be strong and hold on to their faith and beliefs.

"You therefore, beloved...beware lest you also fall
from your own steadfastness...but grow in the grace and
knowledge of our Lord and Savior Jesus Christ."
2 Peter 3:17-18 NKJV

God Commands His People to be Longsuffering

As detailed in earlier chapters, the Greek meaning of 'longsuffering' means 'endurance,' 'tolerance,' and 'patience.'

In Paul's letter the church in Ephesus, he taught that a believer should walk worthy of his calling.

"...with all humility and gentleness, with longsuffering, bearing with one another in love..."
Ephesians 4:2 NKJV

In his letter to the church at Colosse, Paul prayed for the believers to be filled with the knowledge and understanding of the will of God.

"...strengthened with all might, according to His glorious power, for all patience and longsuffering with joy..."
Colossians 1:11 NKJV

In Paul's first letter to his protégé Timothy, he told Timothy that he, Paul, was an example of longsuffering for the believer.

"However, for this reason I obtained mercy, that in me first Jesus Christ might show all longsuffering, as a pattern to those who are going to believe on Him for everlasting life."
1 Timothy 1:16 NKJV

In Paul's second letter to Timothy he commended Timothy for imitating him concerning the attribute of longsuffering.

"But you have carefully followed my doctrine, manner of life, purpose, faith, longsuffering, love, perseverance..."
2 Timothy 3:10 NKJV

Paul also taught that righteousness and holiness should be innate attributes in God's chosen.

"...and that you be renewed in the spirit of your mind, and put on the new self, which in the likeness of God has been created in righteousness and holiness of the truth."
Ephesians 4:23-24 NASB

God Commands Man to be Faithful

To be faithful should also be an innate attribute for God's people.

In Paul's first letter to the church in Corinth, he taught that the gift of faith was required to be saved.

"Moreover it is required of stewards that one be found faithful."
1 Corinthians 4:2 NKJV

The basic Greek word for 'faithful' in the above is *pistis* with several significant synonyms including 'trust,' 'believe,' and 'commit.'

The foundational Greek word *pistis* is found in perhaps the most well-known verse in the Bible as previously recorded when discussing *agape* love.

"For God so loved the world, that He gave His only begotten Son, that whoever believes (pistis) in Him should not perish but have eternal life."
John 3:16 NASB

In Paul's letter to the church at Ephesus, he taught that faith is a gracious gift of God and cannot be achieved through self-righteousness.

"For by grace you have been saved through faith; and that not of yourselves, it is the gift of God; not as a result of works..."
Ephesians 2:8-9b NASB

And lastly, in his second letter to Timothy, Paul taught that a man should pursue not only faith, but also other attributes of God.

"Now flee from youthful lusts, and pursue righteousness, faith, love and peace, with those who call on the Lord from a pure heart."
2 Timothy 2:22 NASB

Summary Statement

God created man in His own image. But man failed to live up to God's image; therefore, God came to earth in the image of man to do that which a created man could not do, i.e. fulfill God's required standard of righteousness.

Thus, God in the flesh fulfilled God's law and paid the sin debt for man so that man could be made righteous before his creator.

Therefore, emulating God's attributes is on-the-job training for the future of redeemed man.

The end result will be that redeemed man will be raised up with an incorruptible body that will never perish.

From the time of Adam, throughout history, man deserved nothing, but was freely given everything.

CHAPTER 7

OBEDIENCE IS MANKIND'S PREDOMINANT RESPONSIBILITY

Typically when the word 'commandment' is mentioned in the Bible, the words 'obey' or 'obedience' will most likely follow. In fact, there are no commandments given by God that don't require obedience.

The Hebrew word for 'obey' is *shama* meaning 'to hear with attention,' 'to understand,' 'give heed,' or 'perceive a message.'

Another relevant word is 'observe' from the Hebrew *shamar* meaning primarily 'to keep,' 'preserve,' 'protect,' 'guard,' 'heed,' or 'regard.'

Therefore, nearly every time the words 'observe' or 'keep' are used, they will typically come from the same Hebrew word *shamar*.

There is, however, one other Hebrew word for 'keep' that we'll see. It is *chagag* meaning 'festival,' 'celebration,' or 'observe.'

God's First Command Was Given to Adam

After God created the heaven and earth, He created all living things in the waters, fowls of the air, and living creatures to roam on the earth.

And on the sixth day God created man in His own image…

"… and breathed into his nostrils the breath of life; and man became a living soul."
Genesis 2:7b KJV

The Hebrew word for 'breath' in the above is *neshamah* meaning 'spirit.' Interestingly another Hebrew word for 'breath' is *ruach* meaning 'wind.'

The Hebrew word for 'life' and 'living' is *chay* with rich meanings including 'sustain life,' 'live forever,' and 'running water.'

God gave Adam dominion over all living things. God also gave Adam all vegetation for food for himself and all other living things.

Then God placed Adam in a garden that He had planted eastward in Eden.

"And out of the ground the LORD made every tree grow that is pleasant to the sight and good for food. The tree of life was also in the midst of the garden, and the tree of the knowledge of good and evil."
Genesis 2:9 NKJV

Then God gave Adam His first commandment.

"And the LORD God commanded the man, saying, 'Of every tree of the garden you may freely eat; but of the tree of the knowledge of good and evil you shall not eat for in the day that you eat of it you shall surely die.'"
Genesis 2:15-17 NKJV

The Hebrew word for 'commanded' is *tsawah* meaning 'establish,' 'constitute,' 'make firm,' 'charge,' and 'appoint.'

The Hebrew word for 'knowledge' is *daath* with several rich meanings including 'insight,' 'intelligence,' 'understanding,' and 'discernment.'

Through the succeeding years God gave commandments to His people; however, His formal, official, detailed standard of righteousness, was not revealed until several thousand years after Adam.

Genesis, Exodus, Leviticus, Numbers, and Deuteronomy

When studying God's commandments and laws for Israel, it is helpful to see the timing of each of the mentioned books that will be used for reference.

In Genesis we learn that Jacob went to Egypt in 1875 BC which began the time of Egyptian bondage. The Book of Genesis ends with the death of Jacob's son Joseph in 1802 BC.

The Exodus occurred in 1445 BC. Therefore, the time of bondage was 430 years, between Jacob's arrival in Egypt to the Exodus.

Moses was born in 1525 BC. He lived for 120 years and

died just prior to the Israelites crossing the river in 1405 BC.

The completion of the tabernacle was the last event recorded in the Book of Exodus.

"And it came to pass in the first month in the second year, on the first day of the month, that the tabernacle was reared up."
Exodus 40:17 KJV

The events in the Book of Leviticus are believed to begin also in the first month of the second year after the Exodus.

Then the Book of Numbers begins shortly after that.

"And the LORD spoke unto Moses in the wilderness of Sinai, in the tabernacle of the congregation, on the first day of the second month, in the second year after they were come out of the land of Egypt..."
Numbers 1:1 KJV

Scholars tell us that the first fourteen chapters of Numbers were written in 1444 BC, or the first year after the Exodus. Likewise from chapter twenty through the end of the book was written in the final two years before crossing into the Promised Land, i.e. 1406 BC or 1405 BC.

The Book of Deuteronomy; however, is different. Deuteronomy is in essence a summation of the previous books in the Pentateuch. It was written in the last month of the forty year wilderness journey.

"And it came to pass in the fortieth year, in the eleventh month, on the first day of the month, that Moses spoke unto the children of Israel, according unto all that the LORD had given him in commandment unto them..."
Deuteronomy 1:3 KJV

Whereas, the laws and commandments given in Genesis, Exodus, Leviticus, and Numbers are specific and detailed, the book of Deuteronomy speaks of the laws in general and the blessing and curses to be experienced for obedience and/or disobedience.

Do not Add or Subtract from God's Laws

When Moses was explaining the statutes and judgments to the people, he stressed that the law had to be followed in full as commanded, and exactly as given. No private interpretation was allowed.

"Ye shall not add unto the word which I command you, neither shall ye diminish anything from it, that ye may keep (shamar) the commandments of the LORD your God..."
Deuteronomy 4:2 KJV

When Moses was warning the people not to be tempted to follow false gods of the nations that God was about to dispossess, he again commanded strict obedience to the law.

"Whatever I command you, be careful to observe (shamar) it; you shall not add to it nor take away from it."
Deuteronomy 12:32 NKJV

Approximately 500 years later, David's son Solomon confirmed that total obedience to the law was required.

"Every word of God is pure...add thou not unto his words, lest he reprove thee, and thou be found a liar."
Proverbs 30:5-6 KJV

Do not Attempt to Reinterpret the Law

Then the people are commanded not to reinterpret God's laws to suit their desires.

When Moses reviewed the Ten Commandments to the people, he stressed strict adherence.

"Ye shall observe (shamar) to do, therefore, as the LORD your God hath commanded you; ye shall not turn aside to the right hand or to the left."
Deuteronomy 5:32 KJV

After Moses' death, God reaffirmed to Joshua the mandatory obedience to the law.

"Only be thou strong and very courageous, that thou mayest observe (shamar) to do according to all the law, which Moses, my servant, commanded thee; turn not from it to the right hand or to the left, that thou mayest prosper wherever thou goest."
Joshua 1:7 KJV

In the current age, is strict observance of God's laws still relevant?

Jesus answered that question via an angel speaking to John in the final Book of the Bible.

"For I testify to everyone who hears the words of the prophecy of this book; If anyone adds to these things, God will add to him the plagues that are written in this book; and if anyone takes away from the words of the book of this prophecy, God shall take away his part from the Book of Life, from the holy city, and from the things which are written in this book."
Revelation 22:18-19 NKJV

Forty Years of Testing to Teach Israel Obedience

Recall that God had given Pharaoh nine opportunities to release God's people from bondage, but Pharaoh hardened his heart each time and wouldn't let God's people go.

As a result, God spoke to Moses in advance, detailing the tenth and final plague.

"And the LORD said unto Moses, yet will I bring one plague more upon Pharaoh, and upon Egypt; afterwards he will let you go from here..."
Exodus 11:1a KJV

God told Moses to explain to the people what the final plague would entail.

"And Moses said, 'Thus saith the LORD, about midnight will I go out into the midst of Egypt. And all the first-born in the land of Egypt shall die, from the first-born of Pharaoh...even unto the first-born of the maidservant who is behind the mill...'"
Exodus 11:4-5 KJV

The Passover and its Significance

Previous to that last day before the Exodus, God had given detailed instructions to Moses and Aaron on how to prepare for that historic event.

"And the LORD spoke unto Moses and Aaron in the land of Egypt, saying, 'this month shall be unto you the beginning of months: it shall be the first month of the year to you.'"
Exodus 12:1-2 KJV

"...In the tenth day of this month they shall take to them every man a lamb...your lamb shall be without blemish, a male of the first year...and ye shall keep it until the fourteenth day of the same month; and the whole assembly of the congregation of Israel shall kill it in the evening...

...And they shall take of the blood, and strike it on the two side posts and on the upper door post of the houses, wherein they shall eat it.
Exodus 12:3b-7 KJV

The people were further instructed to eat the lamb with unleavened bread.

"...and ye shall eat it in haste; it is the LORD's passover."
Exodus 12:11b KJV

"For I will pass through the land of Egypt this night, and will smite all the first-born in the land of Egypt, both man and beast...and the blood shall be to you for a token

upon the houses where ye are; and when I see the blood, I will pass over you..."
Exodus 12:12-13a KJV

Thus, the people were to take an unblemished lamb, kill it at twilight, roast it in fire, and eat it with unleavened bread. The shed blood of that lamb was to be sprinkled on the door posts and lintel of the houses of the people which would be seen by God and save them from death.

"So this day shall be to you a memorial; and you shall keep (chagag) it as a feast to the LORD throughout your generations..."
Exodus 12:14a NKJV

Then on the following morning the people were to leave in haste. That day would begin the seven day Feast of Unleavened Bread.

"And ye shall observe (shamar) the feast of unleavened bread; for in this very same day have I brought your armies out of the land of Egypt; therefore shall ye observe (shamar) this day in your generations by an ordinance forever."
Exodus 12:17 KJV

Also, as previously explained, the word 'observe' in Hebrew is *shamar* which means to 'keep,' or 'guard.' Thus 'keep' and 'observe' may be used interchangeably.

A significant issue relative to the Passover and the Feast of Unleavened Bread is that they are the initial events in God's universal law preceding the giving of the Ten Commandments on Mount Sinai just three months after the Exodus.

The Wilderness Journey Begins

"So Moses brought Israel from the Red Sea, and they went out into the wilderness of Shur; and they went three days in the wilderness and found no water."
Exodus 15:22 KJV

They came to Marah, but the waters were bitter; however, the LORD showed Moses a certain tree that if he cast that tree into the water the water would be made sweet. And so it was.

The wilderness journey would be a period of profound testing of the people's obedience.

"...there he (God) made for them a statute and an ordinance, and there he tested them, and said, 'If thou wilt diligently hearken (shama) to the voice of the LORD thy God, and wilt do that which is right in his sight, and wilt give ear to his commandments, and keep (shamar) all his statutes, I will put none of these diseases upon thee, which I have brought upon the Egyptians...'"
Exodus 15:25b-26 KJV

Then they journeyed to Elim where there was abundant water and numerous Palm trees. After camping in Elim for approximately six weeks they went to a place between Elim and Sinai on the fifteenth day of the second month after the Exodus.

There they complained to Moses and Aaron that they had no bread.

"And the children of Israel said unto them, would that we had died by the hand of the LORD in the land of Egypt when we sat by the flesh pots, and when we did eat bread to the full; for ye have brought us forth into this wilderness, to kill this whole assembly with hunger."
Exodus 16:3 KJV

An Initial Test of Obedience

Then God told Moses that He would rain bread from heaven and the people could gather a certain quota every day, to test their obedience.

At that time God also provided quail for meat each day in the evening and bread in the mornings. If they gathered more bread than needed for a given day, and they left some for the following morning, it would be full of worms.

Then Moses told them to gather twice as much on the sixth day and keep what was left over for the next day.

"...tomorrow is the rest of the holy sabbath unto the LORD: bake that which ye will bake today... and that which remaineth over layup for you to be kept until the morning."
Exodus 16:23 KJV

But alas, some of the people still went out on the seventh day to gather, but they found none.

"And the LORD said unto Moses, how long refuse ye to keep (shamar) my commandments and my laws? See, the LORD hath given you the sabbath; therefore he giveth you on the sixth day the bread of two days.'"
Exodus 16:28-29a KJV

Shortly thereafter, the people set out from the Wilderness of Sin and journeyed to Rephidim, but again there was no water to drink. The people contended with Moses again and asked why he brought them out of Egypt to die in the wilderness for lack of water.

Moses asked God what he should do seeing the people were 'almost ready to stone me!'

"And the LORD said unto Moses, 'go on before the people...take thy rod, wherewith thou smotest the river, take in thine hand, and go. Behold, I will stand before thee there upon the rock in Horeb; and thou shalt smite the rock, and there shall come water out of it that the people may drink."
Exodus 17:5-6a KJV

"And Moses did so in the sight of the elders of Israel."
Exodus 17:6b KJV

The Law Is Given by God from Mount Sinai

"In the third month, when the children of Israel were gone forth out of the land of Egypt, the same day came they into the wilderness of Sinai."
Exodus 19:1 KJV

God called Moses up to Mount Sinai just three days before He gave the law. He told Moses to remind the people that He, God, had delivered them from Egyptian bondage.

"Now therefore, if ye will obey (shama) my voice indeed, and keep (shamar) my covenant, then ye shall be a peculiar treasure unto me above all people; for all the earth is mine.

And ye shall be unto me a kingdom of priests, and an holy nation."
Exodus 19:5-6a KJV

The Hebrew word for 'covenant' is *berith* meaning 'stipulation,' 'agreement,' 'treaty,' and 'obligation.'

The word for covenant above is the same word describing the promises God made to Abraham approximately 650 years earlier.

It is significant to note that we are discussing much more than history; we will learn the significance of these events to current times.

Then Moses came down from God's presence and told the people that they should take three days to consecrate themselves before God would speak to them from Mount Sinai. The people would observe the presence both in sight and sound of God Almighty as He gave the law; i.e., the Ten Commandments.

Total Obedience Commanded

When the formal law was given at Mount Sinai in 1445 BC, total obedience was also commanded.

"Therefore shall ye observe (shamar) all my statutes, and all mine ordinances, and do them: I am the LORD."
Leviticus 19:37 KJV

Notice that the LORD required total obedience, i.e. **'all.'**

And then God told Moses that the people were to make

tassels on their garments to remind them to obey all the commandments, and thus be holy.

"And you shall have the tassel, that you may look upon it and remember all the commandments of the LORD and do them...and be holy for your God."
Numbers 15:39-40 NKJV

However, there was a problem.

"'Cursed be he who confirmeth not all the words of this law to do them.' And all the people shall say, 'Amen.'"
Deuteronomy 27:26 KJV

Hundreds of years later the prophet Jeremiah confirmed that basic truth.

"...Cursed be the man that obeyeth (shama) not the words of this covenant, which I commanded your fathers in the day that I brought them forth out of the land of Egypt... saying, 'Obey (shama) my voice, and do them, according to all which I command you; so shall ye be my people, and I will be your God.'"
Jeremiah 11:3b-4 KJV

It will subsequently be revealed that obedience to the whole law is impossible for mortal man.

The First Commandment

"Thou shalt have no other gods before me. Thou shalt not make unto thee any carved image, or any likeness of

anything... thou shalt not bow down thyself to them, nor serve them..."
Exodus 20:3-5a KJV

The first commandment is perhaps the major source for the woes of the current generation.

The Hebrew word for 'gods' in the first commandment is *Elohim*, and in the present context means 'pagan gods.'

The phrase 'carved image' is from the Hebrew word *pesel* meaning 'carved,' 'cast,' or 'made of wood.'

And the word 'likeness' is from the Hebrew *timunah* meaning 'fashioned,' 'shaped,' or 'appearance.'

Ratification of the Old Covenant

Shortly after God gave the Ten Commandments, He provided Moses with many more details on subsidiary laws and statutes that Moses was to relay to the people.

"And Moses came and told the people all the words of the LORD, and all the ordinances; and all the people answered with one voice, and said, 'all the words which the LORD hath said will we do.'"
Exodus 24:3 KJV

Thus Moses built an altar and offered burnt offerings and peace offerings of oxen. Moses took half the blood of the offerings and sprinkled it on the altar.

The other half of the blood he sprinkled in on the people.

"And Moses took the blood, and sprinkled it on the people, and said, 'Behold the blood of the covenant, which the LORD hath made with you concerning all these words.'"
Exodus 24:8 KJV

This was the Old Covenant ratified with blood as a precursor of the New Covenant which would be ratified with the blood of the Lamb of God.

Moses Was Called again to the Mount in the Presence of God

Shortly thereafter Moses was called to Mount Sinai to receive the two tablets of stone on which God had written the law for the people.

"And the LORD said unto Moses, 'come up to me into the mount, and be there; and I will give thee tables of stone, and a law, and commandments which I have written, that thou mayest teach them.'"
Exodus 24:12 KJV

Moses did as commanded, and he was on the mountain forty days and forty nights.

While on the Mountain, God also gave Moses the command and details on building a tabernacle after the pattern of the heavenly.

"And he gave unto Moses, when he had ceased speaking with him upon Mount Sinai, two tables of testimony, tables of stone, written with the finger of God."
Exodus 31:18 KJV

Even before Moses left the Mount to return to the people, God told him of what was taking place in the camp of the people.

"And the LORD said unto Moses, 'Go, get thee down; for thy people, whom thou broughtest out of the land of Egypt, have corrupted themselves...they have made a melted calf, and have worshiped it, and have sacrificed thereunto...'"
Exodus 32:7-8 KJV

Inasmuch as Moses didn't return when expected, but had been gone for forty days and nights, the people had gotten together and spoke to Aaron.

"...make us gods, which shall go before us; for as for this Moses, the man who brought us up out of the land of Egypt, we know not what is become of him."
Exodus 32:1b KJV

So Aaron told the people to gather all the gold earrings of the people and give them to him.

"And he received them at their hand, and fashioned it with an engraving tool, after he had made it a melted calf: and they said, 'These are thy gods, O Israel, which brought thee up out of the land of Egypt.'"
Exodus 32:4 KJV

Needless to say, God was angry with His people. He told Moses they were stiff-necked, i.e. stubborn.

"Now therefore let me alone, that my wrath may burn against them, and that I may consume them: and I will make of thee a great nation."
Exodus 32:10 KJV

However, Moses didn't become haughty because of God's willingness to make him (Moses) the head of a great nation.

Instead Moses pleaded for the people.

"And Moses besought the LORD his God, and said, 'LORD, why doth thy wrath burn against thy people... wherefore should the Egyptians speak, and say, "for mischief did he bring them out, to slay them in the mountains, and to consume them from the face of the earth?"'"
Exodus 32:11-12a KJV

Moses pleaded with God not to take His wrath out on His people.

"Turn from thy fierce wrath, and repent of this evil against thy people."
Exodus 32:12b KJV

Moses asked God to remember His promises to Abraham, Isaac, and Jacob (Israel), and that He had promised the land to their descendants forever.

"And the LORD repented of the evil which he thought to do unto his people."
Exodus 32:14 KJV

Then Moses went down the mountain with the two tables of stone on which God had written the Ten Commandments.

Thus, within a short period of several months, after witnessing God's power to deliver them from Egyptian bondage, experiencing His power to provide bread, meat, and sweet water in the wilderness, speaking directly to them from Mount Sinai with the Ten Commandments, they did exactly what God had told them not to do in the very first commandment!

"Thou shalt have no other gods before me. Thou shalt not make unto thee any carved image, or any likeness of anything..."
Exodus 20:3-4a KJV

Moses' Response to their Idolatry

"And it came to pass, as soon as he came near unto the camp, that he saw the calf...and Moses' anger burned, and he cast the tables out of his hands, and broke them beneath the mount."
Exodus 32:19 KJV

Moses not only literally broke the tablets in his anger; it was symbolic of the Israelites breaking the law that God had just given.

The calf was also ground to powder and scattered on the water which the Israelites were required to drink.

Moses then required everyone who would not denounce the idolatry to be killed by the sword of the Levites.

"And the children of Levi did according to the word of Moses: and there fell of the people that day about three thousand men."
Exodus 32:28 KJV

Then Moses told the people of the severity of their sin;

however, he would return to the LORD to see if the sin could be atoned for.

"And Moses returned unto the LORD, and said, 'Oh, this people have sinned a great sin...'"
Exodus 32:31a KJV

God told Moses that he (Moses) should lead the people to the Promised Land. God said that He would send an angel to go before him, but He Himself would not lead the people.

"And the LORD said unto Moses, 'depart, and go up from here, thou and the people whom thou hast brought up out of the land of Egypt, unto the land which I swore unto Abraham, to Isaac, and to Jacob, saying to them, "Unto thy seed will I give it." And I will send an angel before thee... for I will not go up in the midst of thee; for thou art a stiff-necked people..."'"
Exodus 33:1-3a KJV

The people mourned while Moses pleaded with God not to desert them.

Moses continued his conversation with God contending that if he, Moses, had really found grace in His sight that He would show it by going with the people.

"For wherein shall it be known here that I and thy people have found grace in thy sight: Is it not in that thou goest with us? So shall we be separated, I and thy people, from all the people that are upon the face of the earth."
Exodus 33:16 KJV

God then told Moses that He would go with him.

"And the LORD said unto Moses, 'I will do this thing also that thou hast spoken; for thou hast found grace in my sight, and I know thee by name.'"
Exodus 33:17 KJV

Had God really Repented?

It had been said earlier that God had repented, i.e. changed His mind.

"And the LORD repented of the evil which he thought to do unto his people."
Exodus 32:14 KJV

God does not really repent, nor change His mind.

"God is not a man, that he should lie; neither the son of man, that he should repent. Hath he said, and shall he not do it? Or hath he spoken, and shall he not make it good?"
Numbers 23:19 KJV

This is an example of attributing to God human emotions and feelings.

Consider also:

"Remember the former things of old; for I am God, and there is none else...declaring the end from the beginning, and from ancient times the things that are not yet done, saying, 'My counsel shall stand, and I will do all my pleasure....Yea, I have spoken it, I will also bring it to pass; I have purposed it, I will also do it.'"
Isaiah 46:9-11 KJV

The Covenant Is Renewed

God then told Moses to cut two new tablets of stone and bring them up to the Mount and He would inscribe on them the words of the original tablets.

"And be ready in the morning, and come up in the morning unto Mount Sinai, and present thyself there to me in the top of the mount."
Exodus 34:2 KJV

Then the LORD came down and stood with Moses.

"And the LORD passed by before him, and proclaimed, 'The LORD, the LORD God, merciful and gracious, long-suffering, and abundant in goodness and truth, keeping mercy for thousands, forgiving iniquity and transgression and sin...'"
Exodus 34:6-7 KJV

"And He said: 'Behold, I make a covenant...'"
Exodus 34:10a

Then God said that He would do wonderful things that had never been done for any other nation.

"...Before all thy people I will do marvels, such as have not been done in all the earth, nor in any nation: and all the people among whom thou art shall see the work of the LORD; for it is an awe-inspiring thing that I will do with thee."
Exodus 34:10b KJV

God, once again stressed obedience to His laws and statutes.

"Observe (shamar) thou that which I command thee this day..."
Exodus 34:11a KJV

"Take heed (shamar) to thyself, lest thou make a covenant with the inhabitants of the land where thou goest...and they play the harlot with their gods, and do sacrifice unto their gods..."
Exodus 34:12a, 15b KJV

Moses was once again with God on the mountain for forty days and forty nights. God then wrote on the new tablets the Ten Commandments.

Also when Moses went up to Mount Sinai to receive the second tablets of the law, God summarized their conversation.

"And now, Israel, what doth the LORD thy God require of thee, but to fear the LORD thy God, to walk in all his ways, and to love him, and to serve the LORD thy God with all thy heart and with all thy soul. To keep (shamar) the commandments of the LORD, and his statutes, which I command thee this day for thy good?"
Deuteronomy 10:12-13 KJV

These two verses are the basis of this book.

Then Moses went down to speak with the people.

"And Moses gathered all the congregation of the children of Israel together, and said unto them, 'These are the words which the LORD hath commanded, that ye should do them.'"
Exodus 35:1 KJV

In his words to the people, God also gave specific instructions for the actual building of the tabernacle as per the instructions given previously.

Purpose of the Tabernacle

When God created Adam and Eve, He dwelt with them in the garden. After their sin, Adam and Eve clothed themselves with fig leaves and attempted to distance themselves from God.

However:

"And they heard (shama) the voice of the LORD God walking in the garden in the cool of the day: and Adam and his wife hid themselves from the presence of the LORD God among the trees of the garden."
Genesis 3:8 KJV

Thus God was with Adam and Eve in the garden.

As we know, because of their disobedience, Adam and Eve were banished from the garden on the East side clothed with animal skins. In other words, mankind was being prepared for God to once again dwell in their presence.

Mankind has through the years emulated Adam and Eve by trying to hide from the presence of their Creator, but God had other plans.

God's Plan Is to Dwell with His People Forever

"And I will dwell among the children of Israel, and will be their God. And they shall know that I am the LORD their

God, who brought them forth out of the land of Egypt, that I may dwell among them: I am the LORD their God."
Exodus 29:45-46 KJV

God's plan for His people is to restore them and dwell with them throughout eternity.

Consider the future time of the millennial temple when an Angel of the LORD spoke to Ezekiel of things to come.

"Afterward, he brought me to the gate, even the gate that looketh toward the east, and, behold, the glory of the God of Israel came from the way of the east; and his voice was like a noise of many waters, and the earth shined with his glory."
Ezekiel 43:1-2 KJV

The 'gate facing east' and the 'many waters' will be significant in the days of the future millennial temple.

"So the Spirit took me up, and brought me into the inner court, and, behold, the glory of the LORD filled the house."
Ezekiel 43:5 KJV

"And he said unto me, Son of man, the place of my throne, and the place of the soles of my feet, where I will dwell in the midst of the children of Israel forever..."
Ezekiel 43:7 KJV

Now let's take a glance of the Heavenly City, New Jerusalem.

In the last chapter of the Book of Revelation an angel gave John a glimpse of the interior of the City.

"And he showed me a pure river of water of life, clear as crystal, proceeding from the throne of God and of the Lamb...And there shall be no more curse, but the throne of God and of the Lamb shall be in it."
Revelation 22:1, 3 NKJV

Those verses are in the far off future; but let's go back to God's presence and dwelling with His people shortly after the Exodus.

"And the LORD spoke unto Moses, saying, 'On the first day of the first month (of the second year) shalt though set up the tabernacle of the tent of the congregation.'"
Exodus 40:1-2 KJV

Then in the final verses in the final chapter of the Book of Exodus:

"Then a cloud covered the tent of the congregation, and the glory of the LORD filled the tabernacle. And Moses was not able to enter into the tent of the congregation, because the cloud abode thereon, and the glory of the LORD filled the tabernacle."
Exodus 40:34-35 KJV

The Original Earthly Tabernacle Was Patterned after the Heavenly

The original tabernacle was the precursor for God's eternal dwelling with His people.

Immediately after the tabernacle was erected, God gave the laws for offerings and sacred feast days.

"And the LORD called unto Moses, and spoke unto him out of the tabernacle of the congregation, saying, 'Speak unto the children of Israel...'"
Leviticus 1:1-2a KJV

The succeeding verses were the beginning instructions for offerings.

It was at this time that God exemplified the sanctity of the blood of the living.

"For the life of the flesh is in the blood; and I have given it to you upon the altar to make an atonement for your souls; for it is the blood that maketh an atonement for the soul."
Leviticus 17:11 KJV

This great truth will be confirmed and applied throughout the Scriptures.

Also shortly after the tabernacle was erected, the Levitical priesthood was appointed and anointed.

The Book of Leviticus also recounts and amplifies laws originating in the Book of Exodus.

Recall also that the events recorded in the Book of Numbers began on the 1st day of the 2nd month of the 2nd year after the Exodus. Recall also that the contents of chapters 1 thru 14 occurred in 1444 BC while the contents of chapters 20 through 36 occurred during the final two years before crossing the river to the Promised Land.

Chapters 15 through 19 cover events between 1444 BC

and 1406 BC, such as subsidiary procedural instructions for certain laws.

Also the refusal of the people to possess the land is described in the earlier part of the book. Death was the penalty for refusing.

Moses' Dire, Costly Mistake

As just mentioned chapters 20 thru 36 in the Book of Numbers were written in the final years of the forty year wilderness journey.

"Then came the children of Israel, even the whole congregation, into the desert of Zin in the first month (40th year): and the people abode in Kadesh..."
Numbers 20:1 KJV

But, once again, there was no water there and the people blamed Moses and Aaron.

Even though this was the new generation, they reacted like their fathers forty years earlier. They mourned and wished they had died with their brothers shortly after their freedom from Egyptian bondage.

Moses and Aaron pleaded with God for advice.

"And the LORD spoke unto Moses, saying, 'Take the rod, and gather thou the assembly together, thou, and Aaron, thy brother, and speak ye unto the rock before their eyes; and it shall give forth its water, and thou shalt bring forth to them water out of the rock: so thou shalt give the congregation and their beasts drink."
Numbers 20:7-8 KJV

Moses took the rod and gathered the assembly together before the rock, and said to them:

"Hear now, ye rebels; must we fetch you water out of this rock? And Moses lifted up his hand, and with his rod he smote the rock twice; and the water came out abundantly, and the congregation drank, and their beasts also."
Numbers 20:10b-11 KJV

Oh Moses, the price you had to pay for disobedience!

"And the LORD spoke unto Moses and Aaron, 'Because ye believed me not, to sanctify me in the eyes of the children of Israel, therefore ye shall not bring this congregation into the land which I have given them.'"
Numbers 20:12 KJV

God told Moses that he could go up to Mount Nebo and look at the land that would become Israel.

"So Moses, the servant of the LORD, died there in the land of Moab, according to the word of the LORD...And Moses was an hundred and twenty years old when he died."
Deuteronomy 34:5, 7 KJV

Summary Statement

No commandment was given to man that didn't require obedience.

God's first commandment was given to Adam, and Adam disobeyed that commandment and ate of the fruit of the tree of the knowledge of good and evil.

Sadly, Adam and his wife were banished from the garden

and denied the fruit of the tree of life. Significantly, God had covered their nakedness with the skins of animals, replacing their own covering from that which was grown in the garden.

Several thousand years later, after centuries of God's chosen nation being enslaved by the Egyptians, God freed them and Israel began their journey to dwell in the land promised to Abraham, Isaac, and Jacob.

At the beginning of the second year of Israel's forty year journey of obedience, God revealed His standard of righteousness in His Ten Commandments.

And not unlike Adam, the Israelites broke the first commandment given by God, even while Moses was in the presence of God receiving the tablets of stone on which God had engraved those commandments.

And significantly, God stressed obedience to all of His commandments.

The consequence of disobedience was illustrated when Moses was denied entrance to the Promised Land.

Subsequently, the tabernacle illustrated God's plan to dwell with His people forever.

Recall the primary Scripture passage found in this chapter.

"And now, Israel, what doeth the LORD thy God require of thee, but to fear the LORD thy God, to walk in all his ways, and to love him, and to serve the LORD thy God with all thy heart and with all thy soul. To keep the commandments of the LORD, and his statutes, which I command thee this day for thy good?" Deuteronomy 10:12-13 KJV

CHAPTER 8

OBEDIENCE WAS NOT AN OPTION FOR ISRAEL

The major division in America, and in fact the whole world, is whether a nation or individual is a believer and doer of God's word, or is a non-believer.

A believer will embrace the reality of God while the non-believer will reject it and live by logic and individual perceptions of truth.

Thus far we have discussed God's commands given to His people to be obedient, including emulating His attributes.

Now we'll discuss general obedience and disobedience primarily in Israel's history which is the benchmark for obedience during the church age which will be presented in the following chapter.

Rewards for Obedience Are Found
Early in the History of Man

Let's go back to the beginning chapters in Genesis.

Recall the sons of Adam and Eve, i.e. Cain and Abel. It

is accepted that God had specified which type of offering would be acceptable based on the covering that God gave to Adam and Eve when they were banished from the garden.

They had tried to cover their sin with leaves grown in the garden; however, God had replaced the leaves with the skins of animals which required the shedding of blood.

The following describes the first blood offering for the atonement of sin.

"So it came about in the course of time that Cain brought an offering to the LORD of the fruit of the ground. And Abel, on his part also brought of the firstlings of his flock... And the LORD had regard for Abel and for his offering; but for Cain and for his offering He had no regard. So Cain became very angry and his countenance fell"
Genesis 4:3-5 NASB

Cain subsequently killed his righteous brother Abel.

Note the similarity of Cain's offering to Adam and Eve's attempt to cover their sin. Both attempted to cover their sins with plants instead of shed blood of animals.

Note also that Adam and Eve were sent out of the garden on the east. That is the same direction that Cain journeyed to and dwelt.

Several thousand years later the earth was plagued with the disobedience of man.

"Then the LORD saw that the wickedness of man was great on the earth, and that every intent of the thoughts of

his heart was only evil continually...But Noah found favor (grace) in the eyes of the LORD."
Genesis 6:5, 8 NASB

God told Noah that He was going to destroy man and life on the earth and that he should build an ark to preserve himself, his family, and two of each kind of animal and bird.

Noah Was Obedient

God told Noah that He would establish His covenant with him. Noah was given specific instructions on the construction and dimensions of the ark.

"Thus Noah did; according to all that God commanded him, so he did. Then the LORD said to Noah, 'Come into the ark, you and all your household, because I have seen that you are righteous before me in this generation.'"
Genesis 6:22-7:1 NKJV

Therefore Noah obeyed God's commandments and it was accounted to him for righteousness.

After the flood Noah came off the ark and made an altar and offered burnt offerings to the LORD. God was pleased with Noah and made a profound statement.

"...I will never again curse the ground for man's sake, although the imagination (intent or thought) of man's heart is evil from his youth..."
Genesis 8:21 NKJV

God proclaimed that even though man's thoughts were

innately evil, He would never destroy him or the earth again. That means that man's righteousness was insufficient and there would need to be something from God to make man righteous in His sight.

Noah had three sons, Shem, Ham, and Japheth.

Nine generations from Shem, Abraham was born.

God Tests Abraham's Obedience

When Abraham's son Isaac was approximately twenty years old, God told Abraham to offer him as a burnt offering.

God referred to Isaac as Abraham's only son. Ishmael was born to Sarah's maid Hagar, and they had since been banished from the home of Abraham and Sarah.

And recall that even though Ishmael was older than Isaac, God had made it very clear that Ishmael would not be considered a descendant of Abraham and thus would have no part in the covenant that God made with Abraham.

What must have been going through Abraham's mind? He was told to slaughter his only son. Who would inherit the promises that God made to Abraham and his descendants?

How did Abraham react?

"So Abraham rose early in the morning and saddled his donkey, and took two of his young men with him and Isaac his son; and he split the wood for the burnt offering, and arose and went to the place of which God had told him." Genesis 22:3 NASB

After several days' journey, Isaac questioned his father.

"Behold, the fire and the wood, but where is the lamb for the burnt offering?"
Genesis 22:7b NASB

Abraham's reply:

"God will provide for Himself the lamb for the burnt offering."
Genesis 22:8 NASB

When they reached the place that God had told Abraham, Abraham built an altar, set the wood in place, bound his son Isaac, and laid him on the wood. Then he took the knife in his hand and was prepared to slay his son.

But the Angel of the LORD called to Abraham from heaven and said:

"Do not stretch out your hand against the lad, and do nothing to him; for now I know that you fear (revere) God, since you have not withheld your son, your only son, from Me."
Genesis 22:12 NASB

Just then Abraham looked around and saw a ram caught in a thicket by his horns. So he took the ram and offered it up as a substitute for his son Isaac.

Abraham, from that time on, called the name of that place 'In the Mount of the LORD it shall be provided.'

What an indescribable reward for Abraham's obedience!

Note not only the location of that place, but also its name.

God Commands Obedience and Condemns Disobedience

Let's progress 645 years after God called Abraham from east of the Euphrates River.

Inasmuch as Deuteronomy summarizes the forty year journey from slavery to freedom, and the period in which God gave the law, obedience to that law was a key issue for the people of the fledgling nation.

Just prior to crossing the river Jordan Moses was reaffirming God's laws and their significance.

"So keep (shamar) and do them, for that is your wisdom and your understanding in the sight of the peoples who will hear all these statutes and say, 'Surely this great nation is a wise and understanding people.'"
Deuteronomy 4:6 NASB

And Moses confirmed that no nation had God so close to them as Israel, and no nation had learned of God's righteousness as did Israel, who personally heard the voice of God giving His law.

At that time Moses stressed the treachery of idolatry and stated that the people should never make a carved image in 'the form of anything, and do evil in the sight of the LORD...to provoke Him to anger.'

Such would call for God's wrath if they did such.

"I call heaven and earth to witness against you today, that you shall surely perish quickly from the land where you

are going over the Jordan to possess it. You shall not live long on it, but shall be utterly destroyed."
Deuteronomy 4:26 NASB

That is just one of many examples of the consequences of disobedience.

Soon thereafter, Moses stressed the necessity of remembering God's laws and commandments. They were to teach their children and meditate on the law day and night.

"So it shall be, when the LORD your God brings you into the land of which He swore to your fathers...to give you large and beautiful cities which you did not build, houses full of all good things, which you did not fill, hewn-out wells which you did not dig, vineyards and olive trees which you did not plant – when you have eaten and are full..."
Deuteronomy 6:10-11 NKJV

"...then beware, lest you forget the LORD who brought you out of the land of Egypt, from the house of bondage."
Deuteronomy 6:12 NKJV

The consequence if they should forget the source of their riches and freedom?

"...lest the anger of the LORD your God be aroused against you and destroy you from the face of the earth."
Deuteronomy 6:15b NKJV

As we present many examples of disobedience and priorities, it is beneficial to compare Israel's behavior with that in America at the present time. God never changes, nor does His standard of righteousness.

God's Standard of Righteousness
Is Eternal and Immutable

God's standard of righteousness has not changed over the centuries, nor will it change. God's plan for mankind was devised before the foundation of the world.

"Known to God from eternity are all His works."
Acts 15:18 NKJV

More than 700 years earlier, God proclaimed that the Bible was a Book of pre-written history.

Recall the following immutable Scripture passage.

"I am God, and there is no one like Me, declaring the end from the beginning and from ancient times things which have not been done, saying, 'My purpose will be established, and I will accomplish all My good pleasure."
Isaiah 46:9b-10 NASB

Moses Reiterated the Blessings for Obedience

"Then it shall come about, because you listen to these judgments and keep and do them that the LORD your God will keep with you His covenant and His lovingkindness which He swore to your forefathers. And He will love you and bless you and multiply you..."
Deuteronomy 7:12-13 NASB

Yes, God loves those who keep His commandments, but the consequences for those who disobey and hate Him are quite the opposite.

"...but repays those who hate Him...to destroy them...He will repay him... Therefore, you shall keep the commandment and the statutes and the judgments which I am commanding you today, to do them."
Deuteronomy 7:10-11 NASB

Moses Reminded the People of their Past Rebellion

Moses then recounts God's mercy and provisions during the forty year journey. He said that God led them through the wilderness in humility to test them and their obedience. He reminded them that God provided water when they thirsted and food when they hungered. Their garments did not wear out, nor did their feet swell during that time.

He further reminded the people that as a father chastens his son, so the LORD their God will chasten them.

The people were told that the nations that were going to be dispossessed were much stronger and mightier than they were. However, their God would go before them and destroy their enemies.

Moses gave more details about the wonders of the new land in which they could want for nothing. But he warned them again to remember the source of their manifold blessings.

"Beware lest you forget the LORD your God by not keeping (shamar) His commandments and His ordinances and His statutes which I am commanding you today..."
Deuteronomy 8:11 NASB

Then Moses told the people that if they continued to

disobey they would perish, just as the people whom they were to dispossess.

The people were not to believe that God's actions had anything to do with the righteousness of the Israelites, but rather He was dealing with the wickedness of the soon to be dispossessed nations.

"Do not say in your heart when the LORD your God had driven them out before you, 'because of my righteousness the LORD has brought me in to possess this land,' but it is because of the wickedness of these nations that the LORD is dispossessing them before you."
Deuteronomy 9:4 NASB

Moses further stressed that God was being faithful to His promises made to Abraham, Isaac, and Jacob.

Moses reminded the people that their fathers went down to Egypt with just seventy persons, and now they are a nation of people as 'the stars of heaven in multitude.'

"You shall therefore love the LORD your God, and always keep (shamar) His charge, His statutes, His ordinances, and His commandments."
Deuteronomy 11:1 NASB

The contents of the above verse are found six times in chapter 11 of Deuteronomy.

The Israelites Had Witnessed God's Majesty and Power

"And know this day that I am not speaking with your sons who have not known and who have not seen the discipline

of the LORD your God – His greatness, His mighty hand,
and His outstretched arm...but your own eyes have seen all
the great work of the LORD which He did."
Deuteronomy 11:2, 7 NASB

This generation was children at the time of the Exodus, and had witnessed God's power over Pharaoh. They witnessed the parting of the Red Sea and the destruction of the Egyptian horses and chariots.

Therefore, Moses reminded the people how God had saved and provided for them in the wilderness, and then he described the riches of the land that they were about to possess.

"Take heed (shamar) to yourselves, lest your heart be
deceived, and you turn aside and serve other gods and
worship them, lest the LORDS's anger be aroused against
you..."
Deuteronomy 11:16-17 NKJV

The Israelites were to teach their children the laws and commandments of God so that their days in the land would be multiplied.

The boundaries of the land were confirmed that it would be from the Western Sea to the River Euphrates.

The Israelites had a choice; they could obey and enjoy God's blessing, or they could rebel against His commandments and experience God's curse.

Has anything changed?

Moses' last Words

Just prior to his death, Moses listed in great detail the blessings if the people obeyed God's word in full. Partial obedience was not acceptable then, nor is it now.

"Now it shall come to pass, if you diligently obey (shama) the voice of the LORD your God, to observe (shamar) carefully all His commandments which I command you today, that the LORD your God will set you high above all nations of the earth. And all these blessings shall come upon you...because you obey (shama) the voice of the LORD your God..."
Deuteronomy 28:1-2 NKJV

Note the adverbs and adjectives to add weight to Moses words, i.e. 'diligently,' 'observe carefully,' and 'obey all' of His commandments.

The word 'blessing' in the above passage has many popular synonyms including 'favor,' 'benefit,' 'peace,' 'happy,' or 'good.'

The people would be blessed in many ways if they obeyed.

For example:

"Blessed shall you be in the city, and blessed shall you be in the country."
Deuteronomy 28:3 NASB

- The people would be blessed in all the land whether they lived in the city or in the country

- The people would be blessed in their offspring, their crops, and their animals
- The people would be blessed in God's provision of food
- The people would be blessed in all of their activities
- The people would be blessed inasmuch as God would defeat their enemies
- The people would be blessed in God's provisions and He would bless them totally in the new land
- The LORD their God would establish them as a holy people

"...if you will keep (shamar) the commandments of the LORD your God and walk in His ways."
Deuteronomy 28:9b NASB

If the people obeyed they would lend to many nations, but they would not borrow.

"And the LORD shall make you the head and not the tail... if you will listen (shama) to the commandments of the LORD your God, which I charge you today, to observe (shamar) them carefully, and do not turn aside... to the right or to the life, to go after other gods to serve them."
Deuteronomy 28:13-14 NASB

But...

"...it shall come to pass, if you do not obey (shama) the voice of the LORD your God, to observe (shamar) carefully all His commandments and His statutes which I command

you today, that all these curses will come upon you and overtake you..."
Deuteronomy 28:15 NKJV

The word 'curses' in this verse means 'vilification,' 'reviling', or 'malediction.' It is just the opposite of blessing.

To begin with, the blessings just listed would be nullified, and instead of being blessed they would be cursed in those same things.

For example:

"Cursed shall you be in the city, and cursed shall you be in the country."
Deuteronomy 28:16 NASB

The Hebrew word for 'cursed' is *arar* means 'to bind,' 'to hem in with obstacles,' or 'to render powerless.'

Perhaps the most familiar use of the word is found in the following early chapters of Genesis when God cursed the ground so as to make it difficult for Adam and his descendants to reap bountifully from the ground.

"Cursed (arar) is the ground because of you; in toil you shall eat of it all the days of your life. Both thorns and thistles it shall grow for you...by the sweat of your face you shall eat bread."
Genesis 3:17b-19a NASB

And then numerous curses are listed for disobedience.

"And it shall come about that as the LORD delighted over you to prosper you, and multiply you, so the LORD will delight over you to make you perish and destroy you...

Moreover, the LORD will scatter you among all peoples from one end of the earth to the other end of the earth..."
Deuteronomy 28:63-64a NASB

- The LORD would send confusion in all they set their hand to do

- The LORD would bring plagues and severe burning fever until He has consumed them from the land they were about to possess

- The LORD would cause severe drought

- The LORD would cause them to be defeated by their enemies

- The LORD would bring on them boils, tumors, and itch from which they could not be healed

- The LORD would strike them with madness, blindness and confusion of heart

- The men could betroth a wife, but another would lie with her

- They could build a house, but they could not dwell in it

- Their offspring would be slaves to another people

- A strange nation would eat the fruit of their land

- They would plant fields and vineyards but they would be devoured by locusts

- The alien in their land would rise higher and higher and the people would become lower and lower...the alien would lend to you, but you shall not lend to him

- Because they did not serve their God, they would serve their enemies

- The LORD would bring a strong nation against them to overtake them

- The besiege of their city walls would be so severe that even the refined women of the people would resort to cannibalism by eating their newborn

- If the people continued to disobey, the LORD their God would bring on them extraordinary and prolonged sickness including not only the plagues of the Egyptians, but plagues that were not even written in the book, until the people were destroyed

- The LORD their God would scatter them among the nations, in which they would not find rest, but would have fear and anguish of soul

The above is just a sampling of the curses to be brought on the people if they would not obey all the commandments of their God.

"So all these curses shall come on you and pursue you and overtake you until you are destroyed, because you would not obey (shama) the LORD your God by keeping (shamar) His commandments and His statutes..."
Deuteronomy 28:45 NASB

If they did not obey the law and covenant, the LORD would remove them from the Promised Land and scatter them from one end of the earth to the other. The Israelites would live in constant fear with no rest or security, and not knowing whether each day would be their last.

This covenant was given in the land of Moab on the east of the river. It was given in the fortieth year after the Exodus.

As Moses called all the people together he stressed that the people had witnessed God's greatness as He delivered them out of Egyptian bondage.

Then Moses said that the LORD had not given them spiritual understanding as yet of His miracles and wonders. Moses added, 'to this very day.' In other words Israel was spiritually blind and would be until the New Covenant is given.

Moses reminded the people of the provisions given to them in the wilderness, and of the defeat of the kings of Heshbon and Bashan, and God gave their land to Reuben, Gad, and Manasseh on the east of the Jordan.

He stressed that God had given His oath with the covenant just like He had in earlier years of Abraham, Isaac, and Jacob. Moses stressed that the oath would extend to their children of the future.

The Major Sin to Avoid

The most tempting sin would be to follow the gods of the nations that would be dispossessed.

"...so that there may not be among you...whose heart turns away today from the LORD our God, to go and serve the gods of these nations..."
Deuteronomy 29:18 NKJV

Moses specifically warned against hypocrisy by proclaiming to be obedient on the outside, but compromising on the inside. Woe to that one.

"And it shall be when he hears the words of this curse, that he will boast, saying, 'I have peace though I walk in the stubbornness of my heart ...'"
Deuteronomy 29:19 NASB

The consequence of such hypocritical vanity:

"The LORD shall never be willing to forgive him...and every curse which is written in this book will rest on him, and the LORD will blot out his name from under heaven."
Deuteronomy 29:20 NASB

When the future generations saw the plight of their nation, they would know it was for disobedience.

"And all the nations shall say, 'Why has the LORD done thus to this land? Why this great outburst of anger?'"
Deuteronomy 29:24 NASB

And people would say:

"Because they have forsaken the covenant of the LORD God of their fathers, which He made with them when He brought them out of the land of Egypt; for they went and served other gods...gods that they did not know and that He had not given to them."
Deuteronomy 29:25-26 NKJV

So God would uproot them in his anger and wrath, and cast them into other lands.

God Will Bring Israel to Himself in the Future

And though Israel will break this covenant also, they will not be forgotten. Praise God for His mercy and grace. He will always keep His word.

Moses tells the people that all will come to pass as outlined in this covenant. They will be sent to foreign lands. The blessings and curses will be experienced exactly as promised, and for the reasons outlined in the covenant.

Israel will have the promise to return; however, returning to God is a proactive thing that God will initiate by His grace.

"..and you return to the LORD your God and obey (shama) Him with all your heart and soul according to all that I command you today, you and your sons, then the LORD your God will restore you from captivity, and have compassion on you, and will gather you again from all the peoples (nations) where the LORD your God has scattered you."
Deuteronomy 30:2-3 NASB

And again, it's all about obedience.

Approximately 800 years later, the prophet Jeremiah records God's words where He promises to enact the New Covenant.

"...not like the covenant which I made with their fathers in the day I took them by the hand to bring them out of the land of Egypt, My covenant which they broke..."
Jeremiah 31:32 NASB

God speaks of Israel's restoration through Ezekiel.

"...I will cleanse you from all your filthiness and from all your idols. Moreover, I will give you a new heart and... I will put My Spirit within you and cause you to walk in My statutes, and you will be careful to observe My ordinances."
Ezekiel 36:25b-27 NASB

Note the sovereignty and proactive acts of God and the impotence of man.

"...I will cleanse you..."

"...I will give you a new heart..."

"...I will put My Spirit within you..."

"...and cause you to walk in My statutes..."

Moses then tells the people that God will put all the curses on their enemies that hated and persecuted them.

Israel's Ultimate Choice, in fact the Ultimate Choice for All Nations

The way to please God is not some far off mystery and secret. It is not beyond the sea or in heaven. But the word of truth is very near them.

"See, I have set before you today life and prosperity, and death and adversity; in that I command you today to love the LORD your God, to walk in His ways and to keep (shamar) His commandments and His statutes and His judgments, that you may live and multiply, and that the LORD your God may bless you..."
Deuteronomy 30:15-16b NASB

Paul references the above verses in Romans 10:1-13.

However, God also says that they will perish if they worship other gods, i.e. idolatry.

"I call heaven and earth to witness against you today, that I have set before you life and death...so choose life in order that you may live, you and your descendants."
Deuteronomy 30:19 NASB

And the results of their returning to God? ...they will dwell in the land which their God promised to their ancestors, Abraham, Isaac and Jacob.

Obedience has unspeakable rewards.

Change of Command

Moses was 120 years old and about to die. He told the people that Joshua would succeed him and God Himself would go before them across the river.

Moses spoke to Joshua in the presence of all the people.

"Be strong and courageous, for you shall go with this people into the land which the LORD has sworn to their fathers to give them, and you shall give it to them as an inheritance."
Deuteronomy 31:7 NASB

Moses wrote the law of the covenant and delivered it to the Levites who were to put it beside the Ark of the Covenant. The priests were to read the law every seventh sabbatical year to remind the people of the terms of the covenant.

Then the LORD told Moses to call Joshua and the two of them meet with God at the tabernacle of meeting where God would inaugurate Joshua.

"And the LORD said to Moses, 'Behold, you are about to lie down with your fathers; and this people will arise and play the harlot with the strange gods of the land...and will forsake Me and break My covenant which I have made with them.'"
Deuteronomy 31:16 NASB

God told Moses to write a 'song' summarizing Israel's future idolatry.

"But I will surely hide My face in that day because of all the evil which they will do, for they will turn to other gods."
Deuteronomy 31:18 NASB

God told Moses that the 'song' would testify as a witness to future generations when the many evils come upon them because of their idolatry.

"Then it shall come about, when many evils and troubles have come upon them, that this song will testify before them as a witness...for I know their intent which they are developing today, before I have brought them into the land which I swore."
Deuteronomy 31:21 NASB

Then after many years, evil would come upon them just prior to their return.

That time would be called 'the time of Jacob's trouble.'

Jesus spoke of that time.

"For then there will be great tribulation, such as has not been since the beginning of the world until this time, no, nor ever shall be."
Matthew 24:21 NKJV

Summation of the 'Song'

The word 'song' really does relate to music, in fact two major synonyms include 'music' and 'singing.' The major purpose of the 'song' was to tell in advance how Israel would react after they had partaken of God's blessings in the Promised Land.

The 'song' that Moses wrote is very comprehensive and is addressed to the heavens and earth so all can serve as witnesses to Israel's response to God's laws and commandments.

Moses begins by extolling the righteous and just attributes of Israel's God. He is called the Rock. The word 'Rock' in this song means 'strength' and 'refuge.'

Then the 'song' proclaims that Israel has disinherited themselves from the LORD because of their disobedience. Moses states that Israel is unwise and crooked because they shunned the very One that made them.

They were told to bring to mind the previous days when the Most High gave them the land promised to Abraham, Isaac, and Jacob. God had set the boundaries of the lands to accommodate the needs of Israel's future great population.

They were reminded that they were nothing until their

God claimed them and protected them as an eagle does for her young.

Their God led them to great things without help from any god of the nations. He blessed them in all ways and provided them with the best of everything.

Their response was that they forsook their provider God who made them and dismissed Him from their lives. Such made their God jealous and angry.

They placed their trust in foreign gods; gods of the nations that they did not know, and they even sacrificed to demons. This was done even after they had suffered the consequences of making a golden calf as their god when Moses was on the mount for forty days and nights; and after the law was given and the first commandment, which was extremely straightforward, was broken.

The people reverted back to idols and false gods.

Such unfaithfulness would not go unpunished. God would bring on them foreign nations to rule over them. That would include Assyria and Babylon. God would 'heap disaster on them.'

They would experience famine, pestilence, wild beasts, and the sword. Consider the fourth horseman of the apocalypse during the time of Jacob's trouble.

"When he opened the fourth seal...I looked, and behold, a pale horse. And the name of him who sat on it was Death... and power was given to them over a fourth of the earth, to

kill with sword, with hunger, with death (pestilence) and by the beasts of the earth."
Revelation 6:7-8 NKJV

God would have totally destroyed them then, except He knew the enemy would take the credit for their destruction, dismissing the fact that their God had chastised them by bringing destruction on them. Recall that the king of Assyria's plan and intention was to plunder Judah in the same manner as he had done to the northern tribes.

God then confirms that He will take vengeance on them in His timing. At that time He will taunt them and say, 'Where are their gods, the rock in which they sought refuge? Let them rise and help you, and be your refuge.'

Then God reveals in the 'song' that in the far off future He will re-gather His people. He will provide atonement for His land and people, while rendering vengeance to His adversaries. At that time the gentiles will also rejoice as the millennial kingdom is established.

Post Jordan River Crossing

"For the children of Israel walked forty years in the wilderness, till all the people who were men of war, who came out of Egypt, were consumed, because they did not obey the voice of the LORD..."
Joshua 5:6 NKJV

The promises that God had made for obedience were fulfilled. There enemies were defeated and the people had rest. The eastern tribes returned to their land.

"Not one of the good promises which the LORD had made to the house of Israel failed; all came to pass."
Joshua 21:45 NASB

Just before his death, Joshua stressed the danger of worshipping foreign gods.

"Now, therefore, fear the LORD and serve Him in sincerity and truth; and put away the gods which your fathers served beyond the River and in Egypt, and serve the LORD."
Joshua 24:14 NASB

Joshua was speaking of the River Euphrates which had been the home of their fathers, i.e. Abraham and his father Terah. Recall, the river Euphrates represents a dividing line between those of the east and those who left that land to inherit a new land under the guidance of their LORD God.

"Now therefore, put away the foreign gods which are in your midst, and incline your hearts to the LORD, the God of Israel. And the people said to Joshua, 'We will serve the LORD our God and we will obey (shama) His voice.'"
Joshua 24:23-24 NASB

Then Joshua died in 1385 BC at the age of 110 years old.

All was well, for a while anyway.

"And Israel served the LORD all the days of Joshua and all the days of the elders who survived Joshua, and had known all the deeds of the LORD which He had done for Israel."
Joshua 24:31 NASB

However, after the generation who outlived Joshua, the new generation reverted to the times of disobedience.

"And all that generation also were gathered to their fathers; and there arose another generation after them who did not know the LORD, nor yet the work which He had done for Israel."
Judges 2:10 NASB

This new generation forsook their LORD God and followed other gods of the people all around them. God was angry and sold them to the enemies.

Nevertheless the LORD God raised up judges to rule them and to deliver them out of the hands of their enemies.

Recall in years past that God had stressed to the people to teach their children and grandchildren the words of the LORD. That premise is so relevant today.

From the Judges to the Kings

Samuel lived at the time when Israel demanded a king to rule over them. The king that God gave them was Saul in 1051 BC.

Samuel spoke at Saul's coronation.

"If you will fear the LORD and serve Him, and listen (shama) to His voice and not rebel against the command of the LORD, then both you and also the king who reigns over you will follow the LORD your God."
1 Samuel 12:14 NASB

All the people and their new king Saul were to be obedient to the LORD their God.

But then Samuel also gave a stern warning.

"And if you will not listen (shama) to the voice of the LORD, but rebel against the command of the LORD, then the hand of the LORD will be against you, as it was against your fathers."
1 Samuel 12:15 NASB

A Word from Solomon on Obedience in Ecclesiastes

"The conclusion, when all has been heard is: fear God and keep (shamar) His commandments, because this applies to every person."
Ecclesiastes 12:13 NASB

The major issue in man's life is to obey the words of God. And for those who think that death ends it all, and all sin is forgotten, hear the following words of Solomon.

"Because God will bring every act to judgment, everything which is hidden whether it is good or evil."
Ecclesiastes 12:14 NASB

Every sin must and will be dealt with at the judgment. At the great white throne judgment, all who are not in the Lamb's Book of Life will be judged on their disobedience and pay the eternal price. Those who stand before the Bema Seat of Christ will humbly own up to their sins which may affect their rewards, but then all sins are banished from the mind of God and will be remembered no more.

Obedience during the Time of the Kings

Even though Solomon was the wisest man in the world, he fell to temptations with foreign wives and concubines who turned his heart after other gods; and his heart was not loyal to the LORD his God, as was the heart of his father David.

"So the LORD said to Solomon, 'Because you have done this, and you have not kept (shamar) My covenant and My statutes, which I have commanded you I will surely tear the kingdom from you, and will give it to your servant."
1 Kings 11:11 NASB

That servant's name was Rehoboam who ruled Judah from 931 BC to 913 BC.

"Now Judah did evil in the sight of the LORD, and they provoked Him to jealousy with their sins which they committed, more than all that their fathers had done."
1 Kings 14:22 NKJV

Succeeding Rehoboam was Abijah who reigned three years ending in 911 BC. He also did evil and was not loyal to his God.

"Nevertheless for David's sake the LORD his God gave him a lamp in Jerusalem, by setting up his son after him..."
1 Kings 15:4 NKJV

Then there were several kings that followed that did right in the sight of the LORD.

Abijah's son Asa was loyal to the LORD.

Asa's son Jehoshaphat did what was right in the eyes of the LORD, however…

Jehoshaphat's son Jehoram was not loyal to the LORD, but rather walked in the ways of Israel's king Ahab. (Israel was the northern portion of the land, while Judah was the southern portion.)

Yet the LORD would not destroy Judah, for the sake of his servant David, as He promised him to give a lamp to him and his sons forever."
2 Kings 8:19 NKJV

Thus, there were loyal kings and disloyal kings in Judah. Let's skip forward a century to King Hezekiah who ruled Judah from 715 BC to 686 BC.

"And he did what was right in the sight of the LORD, according to all that his father David had done…He trusted in the LORD God of Israel, so that after him was none like him among all the kings of Judah, nor who were before him."
2 Kings 18:3, 5 NKJV

Hezekiah removed the high places and destroyed the idols. He clung to God's word and placed his total trust in Him. There had not been a king of Judah to compare with Hezekiah.

Hezekiah was succeeded in death by his son Manasseh who reigned until 642 BC.

"And he did evil in the sight of the LORD…for he rebuilt the high places which Hezekiah his father had destroyed; he raised up altars for Baal…"
2 Kings 21:2-3 NKJV

During Manasseh's reign God confirmed that He would put His name in Jerusalem forever.

"...and I will not make the feet of Israel wander anymore from the land which I gave their fathers – only if they are careful to do according to all that I have commanded them, and according to all the law that My servant Moses commanded them."
2 Kings 21:8 NKJV

"But they paid no attention, and Manasseh seduced them to do more evil than the nations whom the LORD had destroyed before the children of Israel."
2 King 21:9 NKJV

Notice that the kings were held to the Law of Moses given 800 years earlier.

Manasseh undid everything his father had done. He was as evil as his father was righteous to the extent that God issued a warning of judgment.

"...therefore thus says the LORD God of Israel: 'Behold, I am bringing such calamity upon Jerusalem and Judah, that whoever hears of it, both his ears will tingle.'"
2 Kings 21:12 NASB

In previous writings we have listed every king and whether they were obedient of disobedient to God's word. Also listed were the prophets who prophesied during each king's reign. We'll not repeat such detail in this writing.

A Sampling of Obedience Warned by the Prophets

"Yet the LORD testified against Israel and against Judah, by all of His prophets...saying, 'Turn from your evil ways, and keep My commandments My statutes, according to all the law which I commanded your fathers...'"
2 Kings 17:13 NKJV

Nearly 200 years after Solomon, when the kingdom was divided, the prophet Amos spoke primarily to the north, i.e. Israel. There was not one good king in the north, from the division to the takeover by Assyria in 722 BC.

During the time of Amos, Judah was actually in the midst of prosperity under the reigns of Joash, Amaziah, Azariah, and Jotham.

"Hear this word which the LORD has spoken against you, sons of Israel, against the entire family which He brought up from the land of Egypt, 'You only have Me among all the families of the earth; therefore, I will punish you for all your iniquities.'"
Amos 3:1-2 NASB

Then just a couple of years after Manasseh reigned in Judah, Isaiah prophesied to Judah.

"'Come now, and let us reason together,' says the LORD... 'If you are willing and obedient, you shall eat the good of the land...

...but if you refuse and rebel, you shall be devoured by the sword,' for the mouth of the LORD has spoken."
Isaiah 1:18a, 19-20 NKJV

Then Isaiah further tells of consequences of disobedience.

"Who gave Jacob up for spoil, and Israel to plunderers? Was it not the LORD, against whom we have sinned, and in whose ways they were not willing to walk, and whose law they did not obey (shama)? So He poured out on him the heat of His anger..."
Isaiah 42:24-25a NASB

Judah, however, walked contrary to God's standard of righteousness, even though God invited the people numerous times to return to Him.

"I have spread out My hands all daylong to a rebellious people, who walk in the way which is not good, following their own thoughts...Behold, it is written before Me, I will not keep silent, but I will repay..."
Isaiah 65:2, 6 NASB

Approximately a half century after Isaiah, Jeremiah prophesied to Judah just before and during the early years of their deportation to Babylon.

"Thus says the LORD of hosts... 'You yourselves have seen all the calamity that I have brought...because of their wickedness which they committed so as to provoke Me to anger...Yet I sent you all My servants the prophets, again and again...but they did not listen or incline their ears to turn from their wickedness...therefore My wrath and My anger were poured out..."
Jeremiah 44:2-6 NASB

Judah and Jerusalem had reached the point of no return.

There was no way that God would withhold their deserved judgment.

"Thus says the LORD to this people, 'Even so they have loved to wander; they have not kept their feet in check.' Therefore the LORD does not accept them; now He will remember their iniquity and call their sins to account. So the LORD said to me, 'Do not pray for the welfare of this people.'"
Jeremiah 14:10-11 NASB

Then recall when Judah's seventy year captivity was nearing its end, Daniel prayed for God to forgive them for their sins and give them mercy.

"To the Lord our God belong compassion and forgiveness, for we have rebelled against Him; nor have we obeyed the voice of the LORD our God, to walk in His teachings which He set before us through His servants the prophets...Indeed all Israel has transgressed Thy law and turned aside, not obeying (shama) Thy voice; so the curse has been poured out on us..."
Daniel 9:9-11a NASB

Daniel humbly acknowledged and confessed the sins of disobedience of Israel. They had not obeyed God's laws.

"Thus He has confirmed His words which He had spoken against us...to bring on us great calamity..."
Daniel 9:12a NASB

Daniel then acknowledged that God had kept His word regarding obedience to His commandments. Because of

Judah's sin of disobedience God brought on them a great disaster.

Malachi Was the Last of the Prophets

Malachi prophesied from 437 BC to 417 BC, approximately a century after the remnant returned from Babylon.

During those 100 years the Jews had regressed into a level of apostasy and indifference that equaled their sin and disobedience prior to their deportation to Babylon.

Malachi spoke of several of Israel's misconceptions concerning the relationship with their God.

Firstly, the Jews questioned God's love for them. As mentioned in Chapter 1 of this book, God explained that He loved Jacob, and not Esau, even though they were brothers.

"Yet Jacob I have loved; but Esau I have hated."
Malachi 1:2b-3a NKJV

Hate in this verse simply means 'not to love.'

God in His sovereignty had chosen to bless the younger Jacob (Israel) over Esau before they were even born.

God further explained that Esau (the father of the Edomites) could not succeed in anything they set out to do because they did not have the power and blessings of God.

The Jews also sinned by compromising their offerings to God.

"You offer defiled food on My altar, but say, 'In what way have we defiled You?'...And when you offer the blind as a sacrifice, is it not evil? And when you offer the lame and sick is it not evil? Offer it then to your governor!"
Malachi 1:7-8 NKJV

Next, the Jews were desecrating the marriage covenant.

"Judah has dealt treacherously, and an abomination has been committed in Israel and in Jerusalem, for Judah has profaned the LORD's holy institution which He loves: he has married the daughter of a foreign god."
Malachi 2:11 NKJV

Then God says that the Jews were withholding their tithes and offerings, thus robbing Him of His rightful due. By such action the Levites were not getting their required funds to perform their function.

"Will a man rob God? Yet you have robbed Me! But you say, 'In what way have we robbed You? In tithes and offerings. You are cursed with a curse, for you have robbed me...bring all the tithes into the storehouse..."
Malachi 3:8-10 NKJV

And lastly, the people accused God of being unfair.

"You have wearied the LORD with your words; yet you say, 'In what way have we wearied Him?' In that you say, 'Everyone who does evil is good in the sight of the LORD, and He delights in them,' or, 'Where is the God of justice?'"
Malachi 2:17 NKJV

The people were steeped in self-righteousness, and as

such didn't comprehend the holiness, righteousness, or the sovereignty of God.

They thought the wicked prospered while the righteous suffered. The result was that the people thought there was no reason to obey and serve God.

However, God in His longsuffering and patience revealed to the Jews what was to happen in the future.

There will be two classifications for the Jews, and in fact all mankind.

"On that day...you shall again discern between the righteous and the wicked, between one who serves God and who does not serve Him."
Malachi 3:17b-18 NKJV

God and His Standard of Righteousness Are Immutable

"For I am the LORD, I do not change; therefore you are not consumed, O sons of Jacob."
Malachi 3:6 NKJV

God's covenant with Abraham and his offspring cannot be altered; it will stand in its entirety. That is why Jacob (Israel) will not be destroyed but will always have a saved remnant.

"Remember the Law of Moses, My servant, which I commanded him in Horeb for all Israel, with the statutes and judgments."
Malachi 4:4 NKJV

Confirming the fact that God does not change, He again

tells His people to remember the Law of Moses, which was given 1,000 years earlier.

God's standard of righteousness is immutable, and it will be the same standard that will be used to judge the nations when Christ returns.

Summary Statement

Even though obedience was required for all of God's commandments, He graciously offered rewards for such obedience.

It began with Abel who offered the correct specified offering of an innocent animal that shed its blood.

Note that Cain offered that which was similar to the covering of Adam and Eve's sin by offering something grown in the field.

Noah was obedient and was considered righteous by God. Abraham was obedient by being willing to offer his only son as a burnt offering, and thus Isaac inherited the promises God had made to his father Abraham.

Years thereafter, God did miraculous things when He freed Israel from bondage, and He told them to remember what they had witnessed. They had proof that He was God; yet Israel continued a pattern of disobedience.

But God, even in spite of Israel's disobedience, gave them a choice to choose life or death.

"I call heaven and earth to witness against you today, that I have set before you life and death...so choose life in order that you may live..."
Deuteronomy 30:10 NASB

CHAPTER 9

OBEDIENCE TAUGHT FROM THE TIME OF CHRIST

The Cross was the major milestone on the eternal journey for mankind. Man was no longer bound to the law.

Praise God for His perfect and immutable plan.

Up to the time of the cross, sin was atoned for with the shed blood of animals; however:

"For it is impossible for the blood of bulls and goats to take away sins."
Hebrews 10:4 NASB

But God Had a Plan

"Therefore having overlooked the times of ignorance, God is now declaring to men that all everywhere should repent..."
Acts 17:30 NASB

And we've learned that repentance is a proactive step of God resulting from faith which is also a gift of God.

Recall from an earlier chapter:

"For by grace you have been saved through faith; and that not of yourselves, it is the gift of God; not as a result of works, that no one should boast."
Ephesians 2:8-9 NASB

Thus the gift of faith is required in order to please God.

"And without faith it is impossible to please Him, for he who comes to God must believe that He is, and that He is a rewarder of those who seek Him."
Hebrews 11:6 NASB

And in addition, no one will diligently seek Him (Christ) for salvation unless His Father draws him.

"No one can come to Me, unless the Father who sent Me draws him..."
John 6:44 NASB

God does not will that anyone should perish, even though sin was prevalent before repentance.

"The Lord is not slow about His promise...but is patient toward you, not wishing for any to perish but for all to come to repentance."
2 Peter 3:9 NASB

The previous chapter focused on obedience relative to God's chosen nation Israel. The benchmark for obedience for Israel was the commandments of the law. What has changed?

The Purpose of the Law

The law was just a precursor for the only absolute remedy for sin. The main purpose of the law was to define sin. Furthermore, it was impossible for any mortal to fully obey the whole law.

"Therefore the Law has become our tutor to lead us to Christ, that we may be justified by faith. But now that faith has come, we are no longer under a tutor."
Galatians 3:24-25 NASB

Moreover:

"But when the fullness of the time came, God sent forth His Son, born of a woman, born under the Law, in order that He might redeem those who were under the Law, that we might receive the adoption as sons."
Galatians 4:4-5 NASB

Then does 'the fullness of the time' mean that Christ was ordained before time began to be the ultimate sacrifice to pay for man's sin debt?

"And all who dwell on the earth will worship him (anti-Christ), every one whose name has not been written from the foundation of the world in the book of life of the Lamb who has been slain."
Revelation 13:8 NASB

It is so significant to realize that Christ was born of a woman. He was the Seed of the woman spoken of in ages past.

After the sin of deception and disobedience in the Garden of Eden:

"And I will put enmity between you and the woman, and between your seed and her seed; he shall bruise you on the head, and you shall bruise him on the heel."
Genesis 3:15 NASB

Christ was totally man and totally God. His mission included destroying the devil and fulfilling the law.

"...the one who practices sin is of the devil; for the devil has sinned from the beginning. The Son of God appeared for this purpose, that He might destroy the works of the devil."
1 John 3:8 NASB

"Since then the children share in flesh and blood, He Himself likewise also partook of the same, that through death He might render powerless him who had the power of death, that is, the devil..."
Hebrews 2:14 NASB

Several paragraphs earlier we learned that those redeemed from condemnation of the law were declared to be adopted sons of the Almighty.

"Therefore you are no longer a slave but a son, and if a son, then an heir of God through Christ."
Galatians 4:7 NKJV

Praise God for His omnipotence that overcame our impotence.

Obedience in the New Testament Church Age Began with Jesus

The primary word in Greek to describe Jesus' 'obedience' to His Father is *hupekoos* with a rich meaning, i.e. 'easy to be persuaded.'

In his letter to the church at Philippi, Paul teaches that the humility and obedience of Christ to His Father was required in order for Him to pay the sin debt for man.

"And being found in appearance as a man, He humbled Himself and became obedient (hupekoos) to the point of death, even the death of the cross. Therefore God also has highly exalted Him and given Him the name which is above every name."
Philippians 2:8-9 NKJV

It is a well-known truth in the Scriptures that exaltation follows humility.

The writer of the Book of Hebrews also spoke of the obedience of the Son to His Father which resulted in the unspeakable gift of salvation to those who would obey Him.

"...though He was a Son, yet He learned obedience (hupekoos) by the things which He suffered. And having been perfected He became the author of eternal salvation to all who obey (hupakoe) Him..."
Hebrews 5:8-9 NKJV

Paul did use a different word for obedience when describing Christ's obedience to His Father. He used the

Greek word *hupakoe* meaning 'being subjective to' plus being 'easy to be persuaded.'

Paul explained the results of Adam's sin and the consequences, and the obedience of Jesus to His Father's plan to give the free gift of life to those who would be obedient to Him.

"For as through the one man's disobedience the many were made sinners, even so through the obedience (hupekoos) of the One the many will be made righteous."
Romans 5:19 NASB

Commandments Jesus Received from His Father

The primary Greek word for 'command' is *entole* which means 'charge,' 'edict,' 'decree,' and stresses the authority of the one giving the command.

As Jesus was addressing the people on a certain day He was explaining that He was the good shepherd, and the good shepherd gives life for the sheep. He also explained His relationship with His Father and His Father's love for Him.

"...I have power to lay it (My life) down, and I have power to take it again. This command (entole) I have received from My Father."
John 10:18b NKJV

Jesus was revealing His power, and foretelling of His death and resurrection.

In another discussion with the people He was explaining His purpose for being in their presence.

"For I have not spoken on My own authority; but the Father who sent Me gave Me a command, what I should say and what I should speak. And I know that His command (entole) is everlasting life. Therefore, whatever I speak, just as the Father has told Me, so I speak."
John 12:49-50 NKJV

Shortly before His departure Jesus spoke to His disciples and told them of His imminent departure, and then the Holy Spirit would be sent by the Father who would teach them all things, and bring to their remembrance all things that He (Jesus) had said to them.

"I will not speak much more with you, for the ruler of the world is coming, and he has nothing in Me; but that the world may know that I love the Father, and as the Father gave Me commandment, even so I do."
John 14:30-31 NASB

Commandments Taught by Jesus

During a conversation with the scribes and Pharisees Jesus was condemning them for placing more significance on the traditions of men than on God's righteous commandments. The subject matter focused on responsibilities relating to caring for parents in their older years.

"...And why do you yourselves transgress the commandment of God for the sake of your tradition?"
Matthew 15:3 NASB

The particular discussion was on *Quarban*.

They had said that they gave the funds as a gift to God instead of to their parents. They argued that they were no longer then responsible to their parents.

"Thus you have made the commandment of God of no effect by your tradition. Hypocrites! Well did Isaiah prophesy about you, saying: 'And in vain they worship Me, teaching as doctrines the commandments of men.'"
Matthew 15:6b-7a, 9 NKJV

Take note how well His words apply to our leaders of today.

Then again just prior to His departure Jesus gave His disciples several commandments.

"A new commandment I give to you, that you love one another, even as I have loved you, that you also love one another. By this all men will know that you are My disciples, if you have love for one another."
John 13:34-35 NASB

Shortly thereafter, Jesus magnified the above words, but added:

"Greater love has no one than this, than to lay down one's life for his friend. You are My friends if you do whatever I command you...I have called you friends, for all things that I heard from My Father I have made known to you."
John 15:13-15b NKJV

Jesus' Words on Obedience (Keeping)

Jesus predominantly used the Greek word *tereo* which means 'keep' with several relative synonyms including 'obedience,' 'guard,' 'protect,' 'observe,' 'hold fast,' 'reserve,' and 'preserve.'

When Jesus spoke to His disciples the last time, He told them to make disciples of all the nations...

"...teaching them to observe (keep) all that I have commanded you..."
Matthew 28:20 NASB

Note in the Old Testament the Israelites were taught to obey all the law, and Jesus told His disciples to teach all nations to keep all of His teachings. Man does not have the option to compromise the word of God and teach that which he chooses to obey and that which he chooses to set aside.

During a discourse with the Pharisees and scribes, they asked Jesus why His disciples did not obey the tradition of the elders, i.e. they were eating bread with unwashed hands.

Jesus quoted Isaiah where it was stated that hypocrites taught as doctrine the commandments of men.

"He was also saying to them. 'You nicely set aside the commandment of God in order to keep (tereo) your tradition.'"
Mark 7:9 NASB

That teaching should cause everyone to evaluate current laws and traditions to see if they are in line with Scripture. Sadly, we already know the answer.

At another time Jesus cast out a demon. Some of the observers said that He cast out the demon by the power of Beelzebub, the ruler of the demons. Jesus taught that a house divided against itself cannot stand.

A certain woman observer blessed Jesus because of His wisdom and teaching.

"But He said, 'On the contrary, blessed are those who hear the word of God, and observe (tereo) it.'"
Luke 11:28 NASB

Hearing and keeping the word of God was taught by Jesus, and later by His disciples. Such was and is man's primary commandment.

Jesus' Teachings Caused Confusion and Division

As Jesus continued His ministry, He caused much division among the people and leaders.

"So there was a division among the people because of Him. Now some of them wanted to take Him, but none laid hands on Him."
John 7:43-44 NKJV

However…

"…no one seized Him, because His hour had not yet come."
John 7:30 NASB

Jesus responded to His accusers…

"Truly, truly, I say to you, if anyone keeps (tereo) My word he shall never see death."
John 8:51 NASB

That really upset His accusers, and they also said that He had a demon because they claimed Abraham was their father and said that he was dead. They asked Jesus if He was greater than Abraham.

Jesus told them that they didn't really know God.

"...and you have not come to know Him, but I know Him; and if I say that I do not know Him, I shall be a liar like you, but I do know Him, and keep (tereo) His word."
John 8:55 NASB

Jesus continued by telling them Abraham rejoiced to see His day. He was ridiculed because He was not fifty years old, how was it possible for Abraham to see Him.

"Jesus said to them, 'Truly, truly, I say to you, before Abraham was born, I AM."
John 8:58 NASB

The point of this discussion is that Jesus said that if anyone keeps His word they would not see death. Then He said that He knew God and keeps His words. He claimed to be deity and that really caused division among the people.

Obedience after Jesus' Departure

Subsequently as Jesus was teaching His disciples about His departure and the appearing of the Holy Spirit who would succeed Him, the disciples had many questions about the Father. Jesus told them that inasmuch as they had seen Him they had seen the Father.

Jesus then gave them a test of obedience.

"If you love Me, you will keep (tereo) My commandments."
John 14:15 NASB

The word 'commandment' has several synonyms including 'decree,' 'edict' and 'ordinance.' The word also reflects authority of the one issuing the commandments.

If they loved Him, He would pray to His Father to send the Holy Spirit who would abide within the disciples.

"He who has My commandments and keeps (tereo) them, he it is who loves Me; and he who loves Me shall be loved by My Father, and I will love him, and will disclose Myself to him."
John 14:21 NASB

What an unspeakable reward for keeping Jesus' commandments! To be loved by the Father and possess the Spirit within them would be their reward.

Love Proves Obedience

At that point Judas (not Iscariot) questioned Jesus how it could be that Jesus could be experienced by the disciples and not the world.

"Jesus answered and said to him, 'If anyone loves Me, he will keep (tereo) My word; and My Father will love him, and We will come to him, and make Our abode with him. He who does not love Me does not keep (tereo) My words;

and the word which you hear is not Mine, but the Father's
who sent Me.'"
John 14:23-24 NASB

Jesus confirmed that he who loves Him will keep His word and also enjoy the love of His Father. He also confirmed that he who does not love Him will not keep His words. Such teaching was the words of the Father.

What a foundational, profound, test of loving the Son!

Subsequently Jesus explained that His love for His own was as the love His Father had for Him. Again His love for His own is reflected in obedience of His commandments.

"Just as the Father has loved Me, I have also loved you; abide in My love. If you keep (tereo) My commandments, you will abide in My love; just as I have kept (tereo) My Father's commandments, and abide in His love."
John 15:9-10 NASB

It is nearly incomprehensible to fully understand that Jesus' relationship with His Father is likened to our relationship with Jesus, if we love Him and keep His commandments.

One of the most profound truths is that Jesus actually prayed for us who heard and obeyed His commandments taught by His disciples.

"...Holy Father, keep through Your name those whom You have given Me, that they may be one as We are. While I was with them in the world, I kept them in Your name.

Those whom You gave Me I have kept; and none of them is lost..."
John 17:11b-12 NKJV

Yes, we are adopted sons of God the Father and joint heirs with God the Son!

Then Jesus prayed that His Father would protect us from the evil one while He departs to sit at the right hand of His Father.

"I do not ask Thee to take them out of the world, but to keep (tereo) them from the evil one."
John 17:15 NASB

Recall several synonyms of 'keep' include 'guard,' 'protect' and 'hold fast.'

Obedience Taught in the Church

There are several predominant Greek words for 'obey' in the New Testament. We'll list the most common and give their meaning. Then when the word 'obey' is found in the New Testament we'll insert the Greek word that is used in Scripture in that particular passage.

The words we'll use are similar in meaning in many cases. The first Greek word is *peitharcheo* meaning 'to hearken' and to be in 'subjection.'

When Peter and the disciples were brought before the council the second time, they were told again to refrain from speaking in the name of Jesus.

"But Peter and the apostles answered and said, 'We must obey (peitharcheo) God rather than men.'"
Acts 5:29 NASB

Then Peter explained to the council that God had raised up Jesus, who they had murdered, to sit at the right hand of God to give repentance to Israel and forgiveness of sins.

"And we are witnesses of these things; and so is the Holy Spirit, whom God has given to those who obey (peitharcheo) Him."
Acts 5:32 NASB

The second Greek word translated 'obey' in the New Testament is *peitho* meaning primarily 'to assent,' 'affirm,' 'to believe' 'thrust,' and 'agree.'

The Judaizers attempted to discredit the gospel message of Jesus to the Galatians even after Paul had taught them in detail.

"O foolish Galatians! Who has bewitched you that you should not obey (peitho) the truth, before whose eyes Jesus Christ was clearly portrayed among you as crucified?"
Galatians 3:1 NKJV

The Judaizers were persistent and continued to attempt to dissuade the Galatians from accepting the simple gospel truth.

"You were running well; who hindered you from obeying (peitho) the truth?"
Galatians 5:7 NASB

Paul told them that they had started well, but were persuaded to question the truth.

The writer of Hebrews taught that men should obey those who ruled over them, particularly church leaders, inasmuch as all rulers are appointed by God.

"Obey (peitho) your leaders, and submit to them; for they keep watch over your souls, as those who will give an account."
Hebrews 13:17 NASB

Such leaders were held accountable to Christ as to their faithfulness in their duties.

The next Greek word translated 'obey' is *hupakoe* meaning primarily 'compliance' and 'subjection to God.'

The context in the following verse defines the environment after seven were appointed to assist in the business of the church. That made more time for the apostles to tend to the work of evangelism and teaching.

"And the word of God kept on spreading; and the number of the disciples continued to increase greatly in Jerusalem, and a great many of the priests were becoming obedient (hupakoe) to the faith."
Acts 6:7 NASB

In his letter to the Christians in Rome, Paul taught that God's gifts of grace and apostleship produced obedience in believers.

"...through whom we have received grace and apostleship to bring about the obedience (hupakoe) of faith among all the Gentiles, for His name's sake."
Romans 1:5 NASB

Paul subsequently compares the disobedience of the first man with the obedience of the God man.

"For as through the one man's disobedience the many were made sinners, even so through the obedience (hupakoe) of the One the many will be made righteous."
Romans 5:19 NASB

Paul also commended the church in Rome for discarding false doctrine while being obedient to the truth.

"For the report of your obedience (hupakoe) has reached to all; therefore I am rejoicing over you, but I want you to be wise in what is good, and innocent in what is evil."
Romans 16:19 NASB

Then in the benediction of this same letter Paul spoke of the revelation of the mystery of the church made known by the advent, death, burial, resurrection and ascension of Christ. Obedience to that truth produces faith to believe and live by it.

"...but now is manifested, and by the Scriptures of the prophets, according to the commandment of the eternal God, has been made known to all the nations, leading to obedience (hupakoe) of faith..."
Romans 16:26 NASB

In his second letter to the church in Corinth Paul speaks

of spiritual warfare that requires dependence on God to fight such battles.

"...for the weapons of our warfare are not of the flesh, but divinely powerful for the destruction of fortresses. We are destroying speculations and every lofty thing raised up against the knowledge of God, and we are taking every thought captive to the obedience (hupakoe) of Christ, and we are ready to punish all disobedience, whenever your obedience (hupakoe) is complete."
2 Corinthians 10:4-6 NASB

In his letter to the church at Philippi, Paul teaches that the humility and obedience of Christ to His Father was required in order for Him to pay the sin debt to man.

"And being found in appearance as a man, He humbled Himself by becoming obedient (hupakoe) to the point of death, even death on a cross."
Philippians 2:8 NASB

As previously mentioned, it is a well-known truth in the Scriptures that exaltation follows humility.

Paul also gave a scathing consequence on those who choose to reject the gospel of Jesus. However, those who obey the gospel and suffer for their beliefs will find rest.

"For after all it is only just for God to repay with affliction those who afflict you, and to give relief to you who are afflicted and to us as well when the Lord Jesus shall be revealed from heaven with His mighty angels in flaming fire, dealing out retribution to those who do not

know God and to those who do not obey (hupakoe) the gospel of our Lord Jesus."
2 Thessalonians 1:6-8 NASB

The writer of the book of Hebrews also spoke of the obedience of the Son and the unspeakable gift of salvation of those who obey Him.

"...although He was a Son, He learned obedience (hupakoe) from the things which He suffered; and having been made perfect, He became to all those who obey (hupakoe) Him the source of eternal salvation..."
Hebrews 5:8-9 NASB

In Peter's first epistle, he confirms Paul's teaching that salvation, which is a gift of God, produces obedience.

"...elect according to the foreknowledge of God the Father, in sanctification of the Spirit, for obedience (hupakoe) and sprinkling of the blood of Jesus Christ..."
1 Peter 1:2 NKJV

The sprinkling of the blood of Jesus acts as a seal of ratification of the New Covenant.

Peter then teaches believers to abandon former lusts and rest their hope on Jesus.

"As obedient (hupakoe) children, do not be conformed to the former lusts which were yours in your ignorance."
1 Peter 1:14 NASB

Peter admonishes them to be holy as the One who called them.

Then Peter teaches the responsibility of loving the brethren following the gift of salvation.

"Since you have in obedience (hupakoe) to the truth purified your souls for a sincere love of the brethren, fervently love one another from the heart, for you have been born again..."
1 Peter 1:22-23 NASB

The next Greek word translated 'obey' is *hupotasso* meaning 'to place in order' or 'to place in subjection.'

Paul also used *hupotasso* in his teachings.

He taught that those with a carnal mind are not subject to God's laws.

"Because the carnal mind is enmity against God; for it is not subject (hupotasso) to the law of God; nor indeed can be. So then, those who are in the flesh cannot please God."
Romans 8:7-8 NKJV

One of the more relevant teachings in the Book of Romans is that all governing authorities are appointed by God.

"Let every person be in subjection (hupotasso) to the governing authorities. For there is no authority except from God, and those which exist are established by God."
Romans 13:1 NASB

"Wherefore it is necessary to be in subjection (hupotasso), not only because of wrath, but also for conscience' sake. For because of this you also pay taxes..."
Romans 13:5 NASB

Paul compares the subjection that the church is to Christ, so a wife should be in subjection to her husband.

"But as the church is subject (hupotasso) to Christ, so also the wives ought to be to their husbands in everything."
Ephesians 5:24 NASB

In his instructions to Titus, Paul used both words, i.e. 'subject' and 'obedient,' in the same sentence. Titus was to remind the church of their responsibility to obey their rulers.

"Remind them to be subject (hupotasso) to rulers, to authorities, to be obedient, to be ready for every good deed."
Titus 3:1 NASB

The writer of Hebrews states that inasmuch as a believer receives chastisement from his earthly father, how much more he should be obedient to God the Father.

"Furthermore, we have had human fathers who corrected us, and we paid them respect. Shall we not much more readily be in subjection (hupotasso) to the Father of spirits and live?"
Hebrews 12:9 NKJV

And James taught that humility is a precursor to obedience to God.

"Submit (hupotasso) therefore to God. Resist the devil and he will flee from you. Draw near to God and He will draw near to you..."
James 4:7-8a NASB

And lastly, Peter teaches to stay away from earthly lusts and set a good example for the gentiles, so they have nothing negative to say against you.

"...having your conduct honorable among the Gentiles, that when they speak against you as evildoers, they may, by your good works which they observe, glorify God... therefore submit (hupotasso) yourselves to every ordinance of man for the Lord's sake..."
1 Peter 2:12-13a NKJV

'Keep' in the Church Age

As previously mentioned the primary Greek word for 'keep' is *tereo* with synonyms including 'obey,' 'watch,' 'observe,' 'hold fast,' 'preserve' and 'reserve.'

As Paul was speaking in the church in Ephesus he stressed the significance of being worthy of their calling.

"...with all lowliness and gentleness, with longsuffering, bearing with one another in love, endeavoring to keep (tereo) the unity of the Spirit in the bond of peace. There is one body and one Spirit..."
Ephesians 4:2-3 NKJV

All believers should possess and exhibit the same attributes inasmuch as there is one body, i.e. the church.

In the benediction in Paul's initial letter to the church in Thessalonica, he asked again that God equip the believers that they would be prepared for the return of Christ.

"Now may the God of peace Himself sanctify you completely; and may your whole spirit, soul, and body be preserved (tereo) blameless at the coming of our Lord Jesus Christ."
1 Thessalonians 5:23 NKJV

As Paul was teaching Timothy, he stressed that he should live righteously and keep the whole word of God as revealed to him, to be prepared for Christ's return.

"I urge you...that you keep (tereo) this commandment without spot; blameless until our Lord Jesus Christ's appearing."
1Timothy 6:13a, 14 NKJV

Shortly before Paul's death he told Timothy that he was totally prepared to die and meet his Savior.

"...the time of my departure is at hand. I have fought the good fight, I have finished the race, I have kept (tereo) the faith. Finally, there is laid up for me the crown of righteousness..."
2 Timothy 4:6b-8a NKJV

Paul had embraced and kept faithfully the gospel message in its entirety.

James, the half-brother of Jesus, stressed the sanctification and duties of believers. James was in the world, but not of the world.

"Pure and undefiled religion before God and the Father is this: to visit orphans and widows in their trouble, and to keep (tereo) oneself unspotted from the world."
James 1:27 NKJV

Peter, in the introduction to his letter to dispersed Christians, confirmed the mercy and grace of God exhibited through His Son, and described the ultimate reward awaiting them.

Their future reward:

"...to an inheritance incorruptible and undefiled and that does not fade away, reserved (tereo) in heaven for you, who are kept (tereo) by the power of God through faith for salvation ready to be revealed in the last time..."
1 Peter 1:4-5 NKJV

In John's first epistle, he explained the test to know if one really knew God.

"Now by this we know that we know Him, if we keep (tereo) His commandments, He who says, 'I know Him,' and does not keep (tereo) His commandments, is a liar, and the truth is not in him."
1 John 2:3-4 NKJV

But he is not a liar if he keeps the word of God.

"But whoever keeps (tereo) His word, truly the love of God is perfected in him. By this we know that we are in Him. He who says he abides in Him ought himself also walk just as He walked."
1 John 2:5-6 NKJV

John confirms that whatever we ask of God will be given if we keep His commandments.

"...and whatever we ask we receive from Him, because we keep (tereo) His commandments and do the things that are pleasing in His sight."
1 John 3:22 NASB

John teaches that one who keeps the commandments abides in the Father and the Father in him. The proof is the Holy Spirit within the believer.

"And the one who keeps (tereo) His commandments abides in Him, and He in him. And we know by this that He abides in us, by the Spirit which He has given us."
1 John 3:24 NASB

John continues to confirm that whoever believes that Jesus is God in the flesh, and loves the Father also, is a true believer, i.e. a born again child of God. As such true believers and keepers of His commandments will love one another.

"By this we know that we love the children of God, when we love God and observe (tereo) His commandments. For this is the love of God, that we keep (tereo) His commandments..."
1 John 5:2-3 NKJV

Jesus' other half-brother Jude taught the importance of abiding in God's love who gives mercy of eternal life through His Son.

"...keep (tereo) yourselves in the love of God, waiting anxiously for the mercy of our Lord Jesus Christ to eternal life."
Jude 21 NASB

It is all about obedience to the truth.

Then Jude explains that one's ability to 'keep' is also a gift of God.

"Now to Him who is able to keep you from stumbling, and to make you stand in the presence of His glory blameless with great joy..."
Jude 24 NASB

'Keep' in the Book of Revelation

Then in the final Book of the Bible, the apostle John describes those who God will 'keep.'

The devil hates those who are God's people, i.e. Abraham's physical saved descendants or his spiritual born again seed, and will relentlessly pursue them to persecute them.

"And the dragon was enraged with the woman, and he went to make war with the rest of her offspring, who keep (tereo) the commandments of God and have the testimony of Jesus Christ."
Revelation 12:17 NKJV

John subsequently tells of the destruction of the anti-Christ and the future of the martyrs of Jesus. The martyrs of the great tribulation are those who keep the commandments of God with undying faith in Jesus.

"Here is the patience of the saints; here are those who keep (tereo) the commandments of God and the faith of Jesus. Then I heard a voice from heaven saying to me,

Write: 'blessed are the dead who die in the Lord from now on' 'Yes,' says the Spirit, 'that they may rest from their labors, and their works follow them.'"
Revelation 14:12-13 NKJV

And lastly, John records the words of an angel describing the end of the things that are quickly to take place.

"And behold, I am coming quickly. Blessed is he who heeds (tereo) the words of the prophecy of this book."
Revelation 22:7 NASB

Upon hearing these words John fell down before the angel to worship him.

"And he said to me, 'Do not do that; I am a fellow servant of yours and of your brethren the prophets and of those who heed (tereo) the words of this book; worship God.'"
Revelation 22:9 NASB

It is all about obedience to keep the commandments of God, i.e. the entire truth of the word of God.

The Majority Will not 'Keep' the Word of God

In this section we will use four Greek words that describe 'disbelief,' which is the most common synonym for 'disobedience.'

The most frequently used is *apeitheo* which means 'disbelieve,' 'disobedience,' 'stand against,' and 'not allowed to be persuaded.'

The second Greek word that we'll use is *anupotaklos*

which has similar synonyms meaning 'disobedient to authority,' and 'unwilling to be persuaded.'

Then there is *apeitheia* which means 'unbelief' and again, 'unwilling to be persuaded.'

And the fourth Greek word translated to 'disbelief' is *parakoe* meaning 'purposely disobedient,' 'inattentive,' and 'apostasy.'

All sin has its beginning in disbelief, or disobedience.

Jesus summed it up very succinctly in John's gospel.

"He who believes in the Son has eternal life; but he who does not obey (apeitheo) the Son shall not see life, but the wrath of God abides on him."
John 3:36 NASB

There is no partial belief, just as there was no partial obedience to God's laws. Jesus represents the entire truth, and complete and total belief in Him is required.

Subsequently, when Paul was teaching the gospel in a synagogue in Thessalonica he experienced mixed reactions. Paul used the Greek word *peitho* which means 'to trust,' 'to agree,' 'to consent,' and 'to assent.'

Recall that disbelievers noted above were identified as 'unwilling to be persuaded.'

"And some of them were persuaded (peitho); and a great multitude of the devout Greeks...joined Paul...But the Jews who were not persuaded (peitho), becoming envious, took

some of the evil men from the marketplace and gathering
a mob, set all the city in an uproar..."
Acts 17:4-5 NKJV

Note the riotous reaction of the unbelievers. Not much has changed.

Paul spoke of the fate of those who quenched free speech. Free speech in the following Scripture relates to suppressing the gospel message of Jesus which is the total truth, as previously mentioned.

"For the wrath of God is revealed from heaven against
all ungodliness and unrighteousness of men, who suppress
the truth (apeitheo) in unrighteousness..."
Romans 1:18 NASB

Paul then speaks of God's 'righteous judgment,' i.e. rewards for the believers and wrath for the disbelievers.

"...eternal life to those who by patient continuance in
doing good seek for glory, honor, and immortality; but
to those who are self-seeking and do not obey the truth
(apeitheo), but obey unrighteousness – indignation and
wrath, tribulation and anguish..."
Romans 2:7-9 NKJV

Israel's Stumbling Stone

And then Paul describes Israel as a branch of an Olive tree that had been broken off for unbelief. Then he metaphorically tells that the believing church could be described as a branch of a wild Olive tree that might be grafted in and be fed by the root of the Olive tree.

"You (church) will say then, 'branches were broken off so that I might be grafted in. Quite right, they were broken off for their unbelief (apeitheo), and you stand only by your faith. Do not be conceited, but fear..."
Romans 11:19-20 NASB

But if the church was disobedient, they too might fall. If God broke off the natural branches, He might do the same for the church and if Israel returned to their God, and believed, they would be grafted in again.

"And they also, if they do not continue in their unbelief (apeitheo), will be grafted in; for God is able to graft them in again."
Romans 11:23 NASB

And of course, the day will come when God will give Israel the Holy Spirit in the New Covenant and restore them during the Millennial Kingdom.

Then Paul tells the church that they were at one time disobedient to God, but obtained God's mercy as He placed Israel in a stupor for their disobedience.

The day will come when Israel will see the mercy given to the church and will become obedient also.

"For as you were once disobedient (apeitheo) to God, yet have now obtained mercy through their disobedience (apeitheo), even so these also have now been disobedient (apeitheo), that through the mercy shown you they also may obtain mercy."
Romans 11:30-31 NKJV

Paul also feared harm from non-believing Jews, as Luke

did, as he planned to travel to Jerusalem with financial aid for the poor. He asked his believer friends to pray for him.

"...that I may be delivered from those who are disobedient (apeitheo) in Judea, and that my service for Jerusalem may prove acceptable to the saints..."
Romans 15:31 NASB

Again, the non-believers, i.e. the disobedient to the word desired to harm the believers. The non-believers were under the guidance of the evil one who hated Christ and His church, as it is today.

Paul taught the Corinthians that Spiritual war cannot be fought in the flesh. Thus while they walk in the flesh, they must entreat God and His power to defeat the enemy. The great division is between the obedient vs. the disobedient to Christ.

Therefore their weapons are mighty in God...

"...casting down arguments and every high thing that exalts itself against the knowledge of God, bringing every thought into captivity to the obedience of Christ, and being ready to punish all disobedience (parakoe) when your obedience is fulfilled."
2 Corinthians 10:5-6 NKJV

The church at Corinth must first learn and be obedient to the truth without compromise, and then the false teachings of the enemy will be totally displayed and destroyed.

In his letter to the church at Ephesus, Paul also taught that believers were once dead in sin walking under the influence of the evil one.

But Christ made them alive!

"...in which you once walked according to the course of this world, according to the prince of the power of the air, the spirit who now works in the sons of disobedience (apeitheia)..."
Ephesians 2:2 NKJV

In the same letter Paul taught the church to live a life that was befitting for believers. They were to stay clear of all uncleanness. They were to be on guard for deceivers with a 'gospel' made for itching ears.

"Let no one deceive you with empty words, for because of these things the wrath of God comes upon the sons of disobedience (apeitheo). Therefore do not be partakers with them."
Ephesians 5:6 NKJV

Much will be said later about the wrath of God reserved for disbelievers.

Paul taught the church in Colosse to think of things above, and not on carnal things. Such will prepare them for the return of Christ. They were to 'put to death' such sins as idolatry.

"Because of these things the wrath of God is coming upon the sons of disobedience (apeitheia), in which you yourselves once walked when you lived in them."
Colossians 3:6-7 NKJV

It is significant to always remember that believers were once unbelievers and could only be changed by God's gracious gifts of mercy, grace, faith and redemption. All were born under sin.

In his letter to Titus, Paul taught him how to prepare those who would become elders of the church. He taught that all things are pure for the believer, but all things are impure for the defiled and unbelieving *anupotaklos*.

"They profess to know God, but by their deeds they deny Him, being detestable and disobedient (anupotaklos), and worthless for any good deed."
Titus 1:16 NASB

It is all or nothing, there is no in between. Either a person is a believer and pure, or an unbeliever where nothing is pure.

And once again, Paul stresses the truth that at one time all believers were unbelievers.

"For we also once were foolish ourselves, disobedient (anupotaklos), deceived, enslaved to various lusts and pleasures, spending our life in malice and envy, hateful, hating one another."
Titus 3:3 NASB

And then the cosmic conjunction:

"But when the kindness and the love of God our Savior toward man appeared, not by works of righteousness which we have done, but according to His mercy He saved us..."
Titus 3:4-5a NKJV

The writer of Hebrews had much to say about obedience and disobedience.

He stated that believers must persevere in their knowledge of the truth. He compared disobedience to the Old Covenant and its consequences, to disobedience to the New Covenant.

"For if the word spoken through angels proved steadfast, and every transgression and disobedience (parakoe) received a just reward (penalty), how shall we escape if we neglect so great a salvation...?"
Hebrews 2:2-3a NKJV

Later the writer confirmed who it was that could not rest in the Promised Land. It was the rebellious and unbelievers.

"And to whom did He swear that they would not enter His rest, but to those who did not obey? So we see that they could not enter in because of unbelief (parakoe)."
Hebrews 3:18-19 NKJV

And the writer continued by stating that those who believed found rest.

The word 'rest' in this context means 'cessation from labor,' or more specifically the 'quiet abode in the Promised Land after forty years of wandering.'

This example is applied to the 'rest' from the works of the law in the New Testament.

"There remains therefore a rest for the people of God. For he who has entered His rest has himself also ceased from his works as God did from His."
Hebrews 4:9 NKJV

And that rest is for the obedient.

"Let us therefore be diligent to enter that rest, lest anyone fall through following the same example of disobedience (parakoe).
Hebrews 4:11 NASB

Peter also taught about disobedience and the consequences as he addressed the pilgrims on the earth, i.e. believers.

Peter used the unbelieving Jews as examples of disobedience.

"Therefore, to you who believe, He is precious; but to those who are disobedient... 'A stone of stumbling and a rock of offense.' They stumble, being disobedient (apeitheo) to the word..."
1 Peter 2:7-8 NKJV

To the unbelieving Jews, Christ is a 'rock of offense' which caused them to stumble; however, for the believers, He is the 'Rock,' i.e. the foundation of the church.

Then Peter confirms that even believers will be judged; i.e. chastised and purified, but the unbelievers will stand before God at the Great White Throne Judgment.

"For the time has come for judgment to begin at the house of God; and if it begins with us first, what will be the end of those who do not obey (apeitheo) the gospel of God?"
1 Peter 4:17 NKJV

As has been proven by Scripture, the sin of sins is disbelief in the word of God.

Summary Statement

Obedience in the age of the church began with the example of Christ being obedient to His Father. Jesus spoke numerous times of commandments that He had received from His Father.

The church was taught that the law given to Israel was a tutor to reveal the definition of sin.

Then it was confirmed that it was 'impossible for the blood of bulls and goats to take away sins.'

Such offerings for Israel were the precursor for the ultimate payment for sin, which required one in the form of man to pay the price, i.e. death.

Jesus stressed that the same measure of righteousness revealed to Israel was required for the church.

As would be expected, the teachings of Jesus caused much division, especially among the Jews who held on to the concept of attempting to obey the law. As such, the gospel of Christ became a stumbling stone for the Jews.

Jesus revealed, however, that it was impossible for man to totally obey the law. The only remedy was to have faith in the vicarious death of the Son of God.

Jesus further taught that he who loves God will keep His commandments.

Later Paul taught the significance of Israel's history as it relates to the church.

"Now all these things happened to them (Israelites) as examples, and they were written for our admonition, upon whom the ends of the ages have come."
1 Corinthians 10:11 NKJV

CHAPTER 10

THE REWARD FOR OBEDIENCE AND THE CONSEQUENCE FOR DISOBEDIENCE IS ETERNAL

Very simply stated, the reward for obedience is eternal life and the consequence of disobedience is eternal separation from God.

Let's first go back to the initial revelation of eternal life.

Water and the Tree of Life

Let's reiterate what was introduced at the beginning of chapter 7, but focusing on a different context. In chapters 7 and 8 the focus was on obedience, in this final chapter the focus is on eternity.

"In the beginning God created the heavens and the earth."
Genesis 1:1 NKJV

"And the LORD God formed man of the dust of the ground, and breathed into his nostrils the breath of life; and man became a living being."
Genesis 2:7 NKJV

As previously stated, the Hebrew word for 'breath' in the above is *neshamah* with the major synonym being 'spirit.'

And the Hebrew word for life 'in' the above is *chay* meaning 'live forever' and 'fresh running water.'

"The LORD God planted a garden eastward in Eden, and there He put the man whom He had formed."
Genesis 2:8 NKJV

The Hebrew word for 'put' in this verse is *sum* meaning 'to set' and 'appoint.'

Note the proactive actions of God, i.e. 'God created,' 'God formed,' 'God breathed,' 'God planted,' and 'He put.'

Now in the garden were many trees that were pleasant to the sight and good for food.

"The tree of life (chay) was also in the midst of the garden, and the tree of the knowledge of good and evil."
Genesis 2:9b NKJV

'Life' in the above is also from the Hebrew word *chay* as previously defined above as to 'live forever' and 'fresh running water.'

"Now a river went out of Eden to water the garden..."
Genesis 2:10a NKJV

It is interesting that man had access to the tree of life,

but not the tree of the knowledge of good and evil. Man did not need to know sin, or its consequences.

However, we know what happened. The devil deceived Eve to eat of the forbidden fruit and she gave also to her husband.

The results were devastating; they were banned from the garden and lost access to the tree of life. And recall they were banished to the east with new coverings of animal skins. That was the initial signal of redemption.

Fountain of Living Waters Spoken by the Prophets

Approximately four millennia after the garden, God spoke of Israel's restoration after generations of disobedience.

"For I will pour water on him who is thirsty...I will pour My Spirit on your descendants and My blessing on your offspring..."
Isaiah 44:3 NKJV

And as previously noted the Hebrew word 'Spirit' in the above is from *ruach* meaning 'wind' and/or 'the immaterial part of man.'

Subsequently, God reveals His disappointment in His people who forsook the source of living waters for that which could profit nothing.

"They have forsaken Me, the fountain of living (chay) waters, and hewn themselves cisterns-broken cistern that can hold no water."
Jeremiah 2:13b NKJV

Then Jeremiah acknowledges God's words that describe Judah's sin of abandonment of God's gracious provisions.

"Those who depart from Me shall be written in the earth, because they have forsaken the LORD, the fountain of living (chay) waters."
Jeremiah 17:13b NKJV

'Written in the earth' means 'as opposed to heaven.' Again, Judah placed their trust in other men and nations instead of the One who made man and nations.

Jesus Teaches the Fountains of Living Water

Recall when Jesus witnessed to the Samaritan woman at the well. Jesus had asked her for a drink. She questioned why He, a Jew, would ask a Samaritan woman for a drink.

"Jesus answered and said to her, 'If you knew the gift of God, and who it is who says to you, "Give Me a drink," you would have asked Him, and He would have given you living water.'"
John 4:10 NKJV

The words 'living water' means 'eternal life.'

The woman argued that Jesus had nothing to draw water with. She asked if He was greater than her fathers who dug deep wells.

Jesus replied that whoever drank from their wells would thirst again, but:

"Whoever drinks of the water that I shall give him will never thirst. But the water that I shall give him will become in him a fountain of water springing up into everlasting life."
John 4:14 NKJV

The Greek word for 'thirst' above is *dipsao* meaning 'to desire ardently.'

Subsequently on the last day of a seven day Feast of Tabernacles, a pitcher of water was carried from the pool of Siloam back to the temple. The water was to celebrate the rainfall for their crops.

At that time Jesus stood and cried out:

"If anyone thirsts, let him come to Me and drink. He who believes in Me, as the Scripture has said, 'out of his heart will flow rivers of living water.'"
John 7:37b-38 NKJV

Then John explained the words that Jesus spoke.

"But this He spoke concerning the Spirit, whom those believing in Him would receive, for the Holy Spirit was not yet given, because Jesus was not yet glorified."
John 7:39 NKJV

The teaching of living waters was so significant that Jesus included it as one of His Beatitudes.

"Blessed are those who hunger and thirst (desire ardently) for righteousness, for they shall be filled."
Matthew 5:6 NKJV

Fountains of Living Water in the Book of Revelation

The final chapters of the Bible conclude the revelation of 'living waters' introduced in the beginning of the first book in the Bible.

After the 'Day of the LORD' when the enemies are defeated and all things are made new, Jesus said:

"It is done! I am the Alpha and the Omega, the Beginning and the End. I will give the fountain of the water of life freely to him who thirsts."
Revelation 21:6 NKJV

Then we note what John saw in New Jerusalem.

"And he (angel) showed me a pure river of water of life, clear as crystal, proceeding from the throne of God and of the Lamb. In the middle of its street, and *on either side of the river, was the tree of life..."*
Revelation 22:1-2 NKJV

And then Jesus confirms His words that He taught while on the earth.

"And the Spirit and the bride say, 'Come!' and let him who hears say, 'Come!' And let him who thirsts come. Whoever desires, let him take the water of life freely."
Revelation 22:17 NKJV

Jesus Promised Eternal Life to Believers

The primary Greek word we'll use for 'eternal' is *aionios* which means 'endless duration,' 'everlasting' 'eternal rest,' and the 'gift of God for those who believe.'

Interestingly the primary Greek word for 'believe' is *peitho*, which also means 'obey.'

The following verse has been mentioned twice previously; however, focusing on different contexts.

"For God so loved the world that He gave His only begotten Son, that whoever believes in Him should not perish but have everlasting (aionios) life."
John 3:16 NKJV

While in Jerusalem Jesus was performing great miracles. On a Sabbath He healed a man confined to his bed. That angered the Jews, and they sought to kill Him. When confronted by the Jews, Jesus revealed that He was sent by His Father, and a person that didn't honor the Son didn't honor the Father.

"Most assuredly, I say to you, he who hears My word and believes (peitho) in Him who sent Me has everlasting (aionios) life, and shall not come into judgment, but has passed from death into life."
John 5:24 NKJV

Shortly after Jesus provided food for the five thousand, many sought to find Him. Jesus told them that they were more interested in His provision of food than the signs He performed.

"Do not labor for the food which perishes, but for the food which endures to everlasting (aionios) life, which the Son of Man will give you..."
John 6:27 NKJV

Then they asked what works they should do to please God.

"Jesus answered and said to them, 'This is the work of God, that you believe (peitho) in Him whom He sent.'"
John 6:29 NKJV

They said that their fathers had eaten manna in the wilderness. Jesus said that His Father would give them true bread.

"And this is the will of Him who sent Me, that everyone who sees the Son and believes (peitho) in Him may have everlasting (aionios) life; and I will raise him up at the last day."
John 6:40 NKJV

Subsequently, at the Feast of Dedication in Jerusalem, Jesus was surrounded by Jews who questioned Him.

Jesus answered that He had revealed Himself to them but they didn't believe because they were not of His sheep.

"My sheep hear My voice, and I know them, and they follow Me. And I give them eternal (aionios) life, and they shall never perish..."
John 10:27-28a NKJV

Shortly before His hour had come, Jesus prayed to His

Father and acknowledged that He had the authority to give eternal life to as many as His Father had given Him.

"And this is eternal (aionios) life, that they may know You, the only true God, and Jesus Christ whom You have sent."
John 17:3 NKJV

Eternal Life Taught in the Epistles

As Paul was teaching the Christians in Rome about the penalty of sin, he also taught the blessed gift of being set free.

"But now having been set free from sin, and having become slaves of God, you have your fruit to holiness, and the end, everlasting (aionios) life. For the wages of sin is death, but the gift of God is eternal (aionios) life in Christ Jesus our Lord."
Romans 6:22-23 NKJV

Paul taught Timothy about the blessings he had received from God. His teaching was to serve as an example for others to whom Timothy would minister.

"However, for this reason I obtained mercy, that in me first Jesus Christ might show all longsuffering, as a pattern to those who are going to believe (peitho) on Him for everlasting (aionios) life."
1 Timothy 1:16 NKJV

In John's first epistle he was teaching that a person should not forsake the truth that they had heard from the beginning. They were not to be led astray with false doctrine. If they would cling to the truth, they would receive the promise of eternal life.

"Therefore let that abide in you which you heard from the beginning. If what you heard from the beginning abides in you, you also will abide in the Son and in the Father. And this is the promise that He has promised us – eternal (aionios) life."
1 John 2:24-25 NKJV

Jesus' half-brother Jude also spoke of holding tight to the gospel message. If they would abide in the truth, they would receive the promise of God's mercy and eternal life.

"...keep (tereo) yourselves in the love of God, looking for the mercy of our Lord Jesus Christ unto eternal (aionios) life."
Jude 21 NKJV

However, Disobedience Brings God's Wrath

The major Hebrew word for 'wrath' is *evrah* which means 'anger,' 'rage,' 'fury,' 'fierce,' and 'indignation.'

Although God's wrath was evidenced in the Old Testament when His chosen nation disobeyed Him, or when He punished the nations for their treatment of Israel, the wrath that falls upon the unrepentant disobedient will be experienced at the end of this age.

And recall, the 'disobedient' are the 'disbelievers.'

In fact, recall that the great tribulation to come is named after Israel, i.e. 'The Time of Jacob's Trouble.'

Many centuries before Jesus came, as Job was responding to his friend's advice, he gave a discourse on the curse on the wicked.

"For the wicked are reserved for the day of doom; they shall be brought out on the day of wrath (evrah)."
Job 21:30 NKJV

The Hebrew word for 'day' in the present context is *yom* which means 'a point of time on the linear time span.' It is a set time for a particular event; in this case it means the time when God will judge the world with wrath for the disbelievers.

Solomon taught that material wealth will be to no avail at the time of God's judgment of the world.

"Riches do not profit in the day of wrath (evrah), but righteousness delivers from death."
Proverbs 11:4 NKJV

God's Wrath Described in the Books of the Prophets

Subsequently, Isaiah spoke of the day of wrath to come.

"Behold, the day of the LORD comes, cruel, with both wrath (evrah) and fierce anger, to lay the land desolate; and He will destroy its sinners from it."
Isaiah 13:9 NKJV

Then God Himself describes what He will do.

"Therefore I will shake the heavens, and the earth will move out of her place, in the wrath (evrah) of the LORD of hosts and in the day of His fierce anger."
Isaiah 13:13 NKJV

About a century later the prophet Nahum spoke of the day of wrath on the city of Nineveh.

"God is jealous, and the LORD avenges...the LORD will take vengeance on His adversaries, and He reserves wrath (evrah) for His enemies..."
Nahum 1:2 NKJV

Several years later the prophet Zephaniah recorded God's words as He spoke of the day of wrath.

"The great day of the LORD is near...there the mighty men shall cry out. That day is a day of wrath (evrah), a day of trouble and distress, a day of devastation and desolation..."
Zephaniah 1:14-15 NKJV

God's Wrath Confirmed in the Gospels

The major Greek word for 'wrath' in the New Testament is *orge* with meanings similar to the Hebrew such as 'anger,' 'indignation,' and 'vengeful.'

And recall that God's indignation is against all nations.

Early in Jesus' ministry John the Baptist was preaching that the kingdom of heaven was at hand. Subsequently, many came from areas around the river Jordan to be baptized.

Also many Pharisees and Sadducees came to be baptized. John was totally non-politically correct and said to them:

"Brood of vipers! Who warned you to flee from the wrath (orge) to come?"
Matthew 3:7 NKJV

John called them a family of snakes.

He told them that they couldn't depend on their physical lineage of Abraham to save them. He told them that while he baptized with water for repentance, the One coming after him would baptize with the Holy Spirit and fire, representing judgment.

The phrase 'the wrath to come' spoke of the future universal day of judgment.

John recorded Jesus' teachings about the authority that the Father bestowed on Him, including the gift of eternal life to those who believed.

"The Father loves the Son, and has given all things into His hand. He who believes in the Son has everlasting life; and he who does not believe the Son shall not see life, but the wrath (orge) of God abides on him."
John 3:35-36 NKJV

God's Wrath in the Epistles

Paul had much to say about the God's wrath to come on all who would not believe the gospel message and the reality of Christ and His mission.

Paul taught that God's judgment was righteous and

those who disobeyed the word of God and dismissed His mercy and longsuffering in favor of ungodly practices, would bring His wrath on themselves. Man has a choice.

"But in accordance with your hardness and your impenitent heart you are treasuring up for yourself wrath (orge) in the day of wrath (orge) and revelation of the righteous judgment of God..."
Romans 2:5 NKJV

Subsequently, Paul taught another significant truth, i.e. a saint should not attempt to repay an offender who caused him harm. God would take care of that in His time.

"If it is possible...live peaceable with all men. Beloved, do not avenge yourselves, but rather give place to wrath (orge); for it is written, 'Vengeance is mine, I will repay,' says the Lord."
Romans 12:18a, 19 NKJV

While teaching at the church in Ephesus, Paul told them that the spirit of the evil one was working with the 'sons of disobedience.' Then he confirmed that before God's mercy they were all disobedient and subject to the deceit of the evil one.

"...among whom also we all once conducted ourselves in the lusts of our flesh...and were by nature children of wrath (orge), just as the others."
Ephesians 2:3 NKJV

In Paul's first letter to the church at Thessalonica, he commended them for being imitators of the true believers. Then he spoke of their suffering and persecution from the

Jews who forbade them to speak to the gentiles about the truth.

"...forbidding us to speak to the Gentiles that they may be saved, so as always to fill up the measure of their sins; but wrath (orge) has come upon them to the uttermost."
1 Thessalonians 2:16 NKJV

From Prophecy to Reality

In the final book in the Bible, John described what he saw and heard about the wrath of God.

He reported that all men from kings to servants tried to hide in caves from the wrath unleashed on the earth affecting all nations.

"Fall on us and hide us from the face of Him who sits on the throne and from the wrath (orge) of the Lamb! For the great day of His wrath (orge) has come, and who is able to stand?"
Revelation 6:16-17 NKJV

The Lamb will show who He really is.

Just as the seventh trumpet sounded declaring that the kingdoms of the world had been given to Christ and His Father, the twenty-four elders fell on their faces and proclaimed:

"'The nations were angry, and Your wrath (orge) has come, and the time of the dead, that they should be

*judged...' and there were lightnings, noises, thunderings,
an earthquake, and great hail."*
Revelation 11:18-19 NKJV

Then just before the seven final woes, a loud voice from
the temple said to the seven angels who had come out of the
temple bearing the seven last plagues:

*"Go and pour out the bowls of the wrath (orge) of God
on the earth."*
Revelation 16:1b NKJV

And lastly John saw heaven open with a rider on a white
horse.

*"Now out of His mouth goes a sharp sword, that with it
He should strike the nations. And He Himself will rule them
with a rod of iron. He Himself treads the winepress of the
fierceness and wrath (orge) of Almighty God."*
Revelation 19:15 NKJV

Believers Will Be Saved from God's Wrath

As Paul was addressing the saints in Rome, he told of
being free from God's wrath after they were justified by
the blood of Christ.

*"Much more then, having now been justified by His
blood, we shall be saved from wrath (orge) through Him."*
Romans 5:9 NKJV

A significant truth is that true believers will be saved
from God's wrath that He will pour out on the disbelievers.

Paul praised the church at Thessalonica for their growth

in the word and confirmed that their belief and obedience saved them from the wrath to fall on disbelievers.

"...and how you turned to God from idols to serve the living and true God, and to wait for His Son from heaven, whom He raised from the dead, even Jesus who delivers us from the wrath (orge) to come."
1 Thessalonians 1:9-10 NKJV

Jesus Will Be the Judge

God has delegated all authority to His Son.

Jesus' last words to His disciples:

"All authority has been given to Me in heaven and on earth. Go therefore and make disciples of all the nations... teaching them to observe all things that I have commanded you..."
Matthew 28:18-20 NKJV

'All authority' includes being the Judge at the end of this age.

The Jews sought to kill Jesus because He claimed to be the Son of God.

"For the Father judges no one, but has committed all judgment to the Son, that all should honor the Son just as they honor the Father. ..Most assuredly, I say to you, he who hears My word and believes in Him who sent Me has everlasting (aionios) life..."
John 5:22-24 NKJV

After Jesus died, buried, resurrected, and ascended, the church was founded and flourished.

While Peter was preaching to the household of Cornelius, he stressed the authority of the Son, which included being the ultimate judge.

"And He commanded us to preach to the people, and to testify that it is He who was ordained by God to be Judge. To Him all the prophets witness that, through His name, whoever believes in Him will receive remission of sins."
Acts 10:42-43 NKJV

Subsequently as Paul was speaking at Athens, he spoke of God's longsuffering by overlooking sins of the past and appointing His Son to pay for those sons. Thus it was time for repentance.

"...because He has appointed a day on which He will judge the world in righteousness by the Man whom He has ordained. He has given assurance of this to all by raising Him from the dead."
Acts 17:31 NKJV

Who Will Be Judged?

Judgment is universal, as is resurrection of the dead.

We've seen that God the Father has delegated all judgment to His Son.

"Do not marvel at this; for the hour is coming in which all who are in the graves will hear His voice and come forth – those who have done good (believed), to the resurrection

of life, and those who have done evil (disbelieved), to the resurrection of condemnation."
John 5:28-29 NKJV

Thus Jesus confirms that all will be resurrected, and all will be judged.

The writer of the book of Hebrews confirmed Jesus' teachings,

"And as it is appointed for men to die once, but after this the judgment...To those who eagerly wait for Him He will appear a second time, apart from sin, for salvation."
Hebrews 9:27, 28b NKJV

What Will Be Judged?

The psalmists were very clear on confirming universal judgment.

One of David's psalms speaks of God's future and 'soon to come' judgment.

"...He has prepared His throne for judgment He shall judge the world (tevel) in righteousness..."
Psalm 9:7b-8 NKJV

The Hebrew meaning of *tevel* above means 'all the inhabitants of the earth.'

Psalm 96 also speaks of God coming to judge the earth and world.

"For He is coming... to judge the earth. He shall judge the world with righteousness, and the peoples with His truth."
Psalm 96:13 NKJV

'Earth' in the above is the Hebrew *erets* meaning the 'physical planet.'

Then an unidentified psalmist speaks of God coming to judge the earth and world.

"For He is coming to judge the earth (erets). With righteousness He shall judge the world (tevel) and the peoples with equity (uprightness)."
Psalm 98:9 NKJV

Specific Judgments

God spoke through the prophet Joel of His judgment of the nations, and the reasons thereof.

"I will also gather all nations, and bring them down to the Valley of Jehoshaphat; and I will enter into judgment with them there on account of My people, My heritage Israel, whom they have scattered among the nations; they have also divided up My land."
Joel 3:2 NKJV

The nations had best beware of their treatment of Israel. Daniel also spoke of one of the last sins of the anti-Christ was to divide the 'land for gain.'

Have any recent proposed solutions offered by America for peace in the Middle East not focused on a two state solution? Have any present members of congress spewed anti-Semitic proposals regarding Israel?

Jesus taught that a man's words reflect his heart. An evil man will speak evil, while a good man with a good heart will speak good and profitable things.

"But I say to you that for every idle word man may speak they will give account of it in the Day of Judgment. For by your words you will be justified, and by your words you will be condemned."
Matthew 12:36-37 NKJV

When Jesus returns to earth after the great tribulation, He will judge all people who are alive, based on how they treated His people.

He will separate all people; sheep on His right, and goats on His left. The test consisted of the following relative to the sheep.

"...for I was hungry and you gave Me food; I was thirsty and you gave me drink; I was a stranger and you took Me in; I was naked and you clothed me; I was sick and you visited Me; I was in prison and you came to Me."
Matthew 25:35-36 NKJV

The 'sheep' asked when they had done those things.

"Assuredly, I say to you, inasmuch as you did it to one of the least of these My brethren, you did it to Me."
Matthew 25:40 NKJV

Those faithful ones would inherit the kingdom prepared for them from the foundation of the world.

However; all others had an opposite destiny.

"Assuredly, I say to you, inasmuch as you did not do it to one of the least of these, you did not do it to Me... Depart from Me, you cursed, into the everlasting fire prepared for the devil and his angels."
Matthew 25:41, 45-46 NKJV

Notice that while the righteous were welcomed into the kingdom prepared for them from the foundation of the world, the others were sent into the lake of fire prepared for the devil and his angels.

God does not will that any should perish.

James also spoke of mercy shown to others, and judgment to those who show no mercy.

"For judgment is without mercy to the one who has shown no mercy. Mercy triumphs over judgment."
James 2:13 NKJV

Judgment of Believers

Peter taught that suffering is a sure thing for Christians. He added that if one suffers for things he has done, there is no glory in that. On the other hand if one suffers for the sake of Christ, God is glorified.

Recall:

"For the time has come for judgment to begin at the house of God; and if it begins with us first, what will be the end of those who do not obey the gospel of God?"
1 Peter 4:17 NKJV

Judgment for believers is for their edification.

As such, judgment of believers does not mean eternal judgment, rather it means that believers will be rewarded for their strengths and chastised for their weaknesses. The chastisement is meant to strengthen the believers.

Perhaps the most significant judgment for believers is the Bema Seat of Christ. At that judgment, rewards or chastisement will be given according to how one used the gifts he had been given. All believers will stand before the Bema Seat of Christ.

It should be the believer's objective that their life is well pleasing to Christ.

"For we must all appear before the judgment seat of Christ, that each one may receive the things done in the body, according to what he has done, whether good or bad."
2 Corinthians 5:10 NKJV

The term 'Bema' is in reference to an elevated platform where athletes would receive their prize or crowns for excellent performance.

Each will be evaluated by their actions during their life as a believer, whether they glorified God, or themselves. Consequence for sin was not the issue; that was taken care of on the cross.

Paul taught the significance of listening to one's conscience which reflects what is in one's heart. Even without knowing the law, God's law is written in their hearts.

"...who show the work of the law written in their hearts, their conscience also bearing witness...accusing or else excusing them in the day when God will judge the secrets of men by Jesus Christ..."
Romans 2:15-16 NKJV

Paul also taught that Christians are stewards of the knowledge of God, and an individual is not capable of judging another.

"Therefore judge nothing before the time, until the Lord comes, who will both bring to light the hidden things of darkness and reveal the motives of the hearts."
1 Corinthians 4:5 NKJV

John taught that true love for God will remove fear in the judgment, inasmuch as God is love and believers will be imitating Him. In other words, true love is evidence of justification.

"Love has been perfected among us in this: that we may have boldness in the Day of Judgment; because as He is, so are we in this world."
1 John 4:17 NKJV

John went on to say that if one has fear of the judgment, he does not really have love in his heart.

A millennium before the church, the wisest man in the world was King Solomon. He summed up the topic of judgment very succinctly as previously stated.

"Let us hear the conclusion of the whole matter: Fear (revere) God and keep His commandments, for this is man's

all. For God will bring every work into judgment, including every secret thing, whether good or evil."
Ecclesiastes 12:13-14 NKJV

The Day of Judgment in the Bible Is Expressed in Varied Terms

The most frequently used words describing the Day of Judgment are 'The Day of the LORD.' Also found in Scripture are 'Day of Wrath,' 'Day of Destruction,' and 'Day of Calamity.'

The word 'day' in this context is the Hebrew *yom* which means 'a period of time' or 'a number of days' in which pre-appointed events take place. Time is a linear function where points on the time span define 'when' while the distance between two points on the time span defines 'how long.'

The time dimension was initiated in creation for the benefit of man.

"Then God said, 'Let there be lights in the firmament of the heavens to divide the day from the night; and let them be for signs and seasons, and for days and years.'"
Genesis 1:14 NKJV

The Hebrew word for 'seasons' is *moedh* meaning 'appointment.' This would teach man how to obey God's commandments to celebrate certain festivals at the appointed time.

When New Jerusalem descends to earth, the sun will not be needed because the glory of God will be the light.

Likewise, there will no longer be the need for the time dimension.

God Will Deal with Man's Disobedience at 'The Day of the LORD'

Isaiah describes that 'soon to be' dark time in mankind's pre-written history.

"Come near, you nations, to hear; and heed, you people! Let the earth hear, and all that is in it, the world and all things that come forth from it. For the indignation of the LORD is against all nations, and His fury against all their armies...He has given them over to the slaughter."
Isaiah 34:1-2 NKJV

The Hebrew word for 'indignation' is *qetseph*. It is the strongest Hebrew word used to describe 'anger' and 'fury.'

"For it is the day of the LORD's vengeance, the year of recompense for the cause of Zion."
Isaiah 34:8 NKJV

The Hebrew word for 'vengeance' is *naqam* meaning 'revenge,' 'retaliation,' and 'punishment." The Hebrew word for 'recompense' is *shillum* meaning 'retribution.'

Other Prophets Spoke of 'The Day of the LORD'

The earliest of the prophets was Obadiah who prophesied about Edom between 850 BC and 840 BC.

Many prophecies have both short term application and end time applications. When the phrase 'Day of the LORD' is used, it will undoubtedly apply to the future day of God's dealing with man during the 70th week.

"For the day of the LORD upon all the nations is near; as you have done, it shall be done to you; your reprisal shall return upon you own head."
Obadiah 15 NKJV

The Hebrew word for 'reprisal' is *gmuwl* also meaning 'recompense.'

And Obadiah wrote approximately 100 years before Isaiah. We'll see that the prophets had nearly identical messages.

The prophet Joel followed Obadiah, and had much to say about the 'Day of the LORD.'

"Alas for the day! For the day of the LORD is at hand, it shall come as destruction from the Almighty."
Joel 1:15 NKJV

The Hebrew word for 'destruction' is *shodh* meaning 'violence.'

Remember, God is not limited to the time dimension. The Hebrew word for 'at hand' is *qarob* meaning 'approaching.'

"Blow the trumpet in Zion, and sound an alarm in My holy mountain! Let all the inhabitants of the land tremble; for the day of the LORD is coming, for it is at hand: a day of darkness and gloominess..."
Joel 2:1-2a NKJV

Joel offers more detail on that great time and event.

"The sun shall be turned into darkness, and the moon into blood, before the coming of the great and awesome day of the LORD."
Joel 2:31 NKJV

The apostle John used similar wording when describing week 70 in the Book of Revelation.

"Multitudes, multitudes in the valley of decision! For the day of the LORD is near in the valley of decision."
Joel 3:14 NKJV

The 'valley of decision' is the 'Valley of Jehoshaphat' where the judgment will be carried out.

Isaiah declared that the proud would fall in that great day.

"The lofty looks of man shall be humbled, the haughtiness of men shall be bowed down, and the LORD alone shall be exalted in that day. For the day of the LORD of hosts shall come upon everything proud and lofty..."
Isaiah 2:11-12 NKJV

Isaiah subsequently speaks of the impending fall of Babylon and then extends that warning to the near future 'Day of the LORD.' Again Isaiah points out the fall of the proud.

"Behold, the day of the LORD comes, cruel, with both wrath and fierce anger...I will punish the world for its evil, and the wicked for their iniquity; I will halt the arrogance of the proud, and will lay low the haughtiness of the terrible

(tyrants)...In the wrath of the LORD of hosts and in the day of His fierce anger."
Isaiah 13:9, 11, 13b NKJV

All who consider only the love of God had best take note.

Zechariah prophesied between 520 BC and 470 BC. He spoke of the future when God would bring the nations to Jerusalem to plunder them. Then He will intervene to rescue them after their punishment.

"Behold, the day of the LORD is coming...for I will gather all the nations to battle against Jerusalem; the city shall be taken...but the remnant of the people shall not be cut off from the city... Then the LORD will go forth and fight against those nations..."
Zechariah 14:1-3 NKJV

Recall the 'Day of the LORD' is called 'The time of Jacob's trouble.' God will deal with Israel in accordance with their centuries of disobedience. However, He will then join in the battle and rescue His chosen people from total destruction.

And remember; only a remnant of His chosen will be saved.

The final prophet is Malachi, and he also spoke of the 'Day of the LORD.'

"Behold, I will send you Elijah the prophet before the coming of the great and dreadful day of the LORD."
Malachi 4:5 NKJV

Malachi presented a ray of hope fulfilled in the New Testament.

"But I say to you that Elijah has come already...Then the disciples understood that He spoke to them of John the Baptist."
Matthew 17:12a, 13 NKJV

New Testament References to the 'Day of the LORD'

Zechariah confirmed that only a remnant of God's chosen nation of Israel would escape the wrath of God.

Jesus proclaimed that same truth relative to the church.

Recall His final words in His sermon on the mount regarding life or death.

"Enter by the narrow gate; for wide is the gate and broad is the way that leads to destruction, and there are many who go in by it. Because narrow is the gate and difficult is the way which leads to life, and there are few who find it."
Matthew 7:13-14 NKJV

The Greek word used for 'destruction' in these verses is *apoleia* which means 'an end of life' and 'death.' 'Life' in the above is from the Greek word *zoe* and means 'eternal life.'

Paul had much to say about the 'Day of the LORD' in his letters to the church at Thessalonica.

"For you yourselves know perfectly that the day of the Lord so comes as a thief in the night. For when they say,

'Peace and safety!' then sudden destruction comes up them..."
1 Thessalonians 5:2-3 NKJV

The Greek word for 'destruction' in these verses is *olethros* meaning 'divine punishment' or 'kill.'

False prophets in the time of Jeremiah also claimed that Israel would have peace and safety. God identified them as false prophets and He told Jeremiah not to pray for those people; they had passed the point of no return and judgment was imminent.

Does that sound familiar to some of the boasting of today?

In his second letter to the church at Thessalonica, Paul commended the church for their endurance during times of persecutions and tribulations.

He then told them of the future of their persecutors.

"...since it is a righteous thing with God to repay with tribulation those who trouble you...These shall be punished with everlasting destruction (olethros) from the presence of the Lord...when He comes, in that Day..."
2 Thessalonians 1:6, 9 NKJV

And lastly Peter wrote to dispersed believers, warning of the approaching Day of Judgment.

"But the heavens and the earth which are now preserved by the same word, are reserved for fire until the day of judgment and perdition of ungodly men."
2 Peter 3:7 NKJV

The Greek for 'preserved' is *tereo* meaning 'to keep in store unto the day of judgment.'

The meaning of 'reserved' is also from the same Greek word *tereo*.

The heavens and earth will be judged as it was in Noah's time; there was ample warning then and now. The future judgment is a sure thing to occur in God's timing.

"But the day of the Lord will come as a thief in the night, in which the heavens will pass away with a great noise and the elements will melt with fervent heat; both the earth and the works that are in it will be burned up."
2 Peter 3:10 NKJV

Following the 'Day of the LORD,' the earth will not be destroyed, or cease to be, but rather will be renewed for eternity.

The future 'Day of the Lord' and God's righteous judgment is an absolute certainty, and yet it is not a topic of discussion in the world, in America, and sadly in most churches.

Oh how we wish that America would take God seriously!

Summary Statement

The end of the journey for believers is eternal life represented by 'fountains of living waters.'

It all goes back to the rivers that watered the garden and the tree of life.

When God breathed life into Adam, the word 'life' means 'live forever,' and 'fresh running water.'

The word 'breathed,' or 'breath,' means 'spirit.'

The Prophet Jeremiah spoke of 'the fountain of living water' referencing the Spirit that would be given to the remnant of Israel in the future.

Subsequently, Jesus also taught that the 'living water' that He would give was the Spirit of God.

Those with the 'Spirit' would inherit eternal life.

Those who would reject God's free gift of living water would taste of God's wrath, which would also have eternal consequences.

God's wrath is succinctly expressed in 'the Day of the LORD' which is the time of judgment of the nations and is approaching quickly at the end of the age of the church, which Paul defines as the 'end of the ages.'

And never forget God's offer to all nations and individuals.

"I call heaven and earth as witnesses today against you, that I have set before you life and death, blessing and cursing; therefore choose life..."
Deuteronomy 30:19 NKJV

But sadly, the vast majority of the world's population will reject God's gracious gift of life.

Printed in the United States
by Baker & Taylor Publisher Services